Involving Community
Members in
Focus Groups

Richard A. Krueger · Jean A. King

Involving Community Members in Focus Groups

Focus Group Kit **5**

SAGE Publications
International Educational and Professional Publisher
Thousand Oaks London New Delhi

For information:

SAGE Publications, Inc.
2455 Teller Road
Thousand Oaks, California 91320
E-mail: order@sagepub.com

SAGE Publications Ltd.
6 Bonhill Street
London EC2A 4PU
United Kingdom

SAGE Publications India Pvt. Ltd.
M-32 Market
Greater Kailash I
New Delhi 110 048 India

Printed in the United States of America

Library of Congress Cataloging-in-Publication Data

Morgan, David L., Krueger, Richard A.
    The focus group kit.
        p.   cm.
    Includes bibliographical references and indexes.
    Contents: v. 1. The focus group guidebook/David L. Morgan.   v. 2. Planning focus groups/David L. Morgan.   v. 3. Developing questions for focus groups/Richard A. Krueger. v. 4. Moderating focus groups/Richard A. Krueger.   v. 5. Involving community members in focus groups/Richard A. Krueger, Jean A. King.   v. 6. Analyzing and reporting focus group results/Richard A. Krueger.

ISBN 0-7619-0760-2 (pbk.: The focus group kit: alk. paper)

1. Focus groups.   I. Title.   II. Series.   III. Morgan, David L.   IV. Krueger, Richard A.

H61.28K778 1997
001.4'33—dc21   97-21135

ISBN 0-7619-0818-8 (v. 1 pbk.)
ISBN 0-7619-0817-X (v. 2 pbk.)
ISBN 0-7619-0819-6 (v. 3 pbk.)
ISBN 0-7619-0821-8 (v. 4 pbk.)
ISBN 0-7619-0820-X (v. 5 pbk.)
ISBN 0-7619-0816-1 (v. 6 pbk.)

This book is printed on acid-free paper.

99   00   01   02   03   10   9   8   7   6   5   4

Acquiring Editor:	Marquita Flemming
Editorial Assistant:	Frances Borghi
Production Editor:	Diana E. Axelsen
Production Assistant:	Karen Wiley
Typesetter/Designer:	Janelle LeMaster
Cover Designer:	Ravi Balasuriya
Cover Illustration:	Anahid Moradkhan
Print Buyer:	Anna Chin

Table of Contents

Acknowledgments

This book would not have been possible without the support of scores ofcommunities, neighborhoods, schools, councils, boards, and groups who have tried these ideas, suggested improvements, and given us feedback. Over the past ten years we have "given away" focus groups to many others. As we've shared, we've learned. We use the word *share* because the word *taught* just doesn't seem appropriate—more often we were the students.

A number of dedicated people helped along the way. Among our teachers were Bonnie Bray, Carol Bryant, Carol Burtness, Leonard Covello, Sue Damme, Wayne Erickson, Sue Gehrz, Gretchen Griffin, Mike Huerdh, Barb Kalina, Karen Lawson, Pam McCarthy, Mary Montagne, Ed Nelson, Mark Nunberg, Linda Prevorrow, Ray Rist, and Rhonda Wiley-Jones.

David Morgan, friend and valued colleague, invited us to assist in the preparation of this collection of books and has been invaluable in offering suggestions and strategies that clarify the writing and presentation of ideas.

The production quality was improved by Susan Wladaver-Morgan, who offered editing suggestions. The staff at Sage Publications continually were most helpful. Their editors were encouraging, creative, and willing to take risks. Special thanks to Diana Axelsen, Ravi Balasuriya, Marquita Flemming, and C. Deborah Laughton, for eagerly contributing their talents.

A good book is one that touches us in several ways. It should be serious, yet funny. It should be challenging, yet comfortable. It should raise the level of thought. But most of all, it should be fun to read. The best test is if you read more than what you intended. Our hope that this book does that for you. May you find the insight, the seriousness, the guiding principles and the humor in this volume.

Introduction to the Focus Group Kit

We welcome you to this series of books on focus group interviewing. We hope that you find this series helpful. In this section we would like to tell you a bit about our past work with focus groups, the factors that led to the creation of this series, and an overview of how the book is organized.

We began our studies of focus group interviewing about the same time. Our academic backgrounds were different (David in sociology and Richard in program evaluation), and yet we were both drawn to focus group interviewing in the 1980s. We both had books published in 1988 on focus group interviewing that resulted from our research and practice with the methodology. At that time, we were unaware of one another's work and were pleased to begin a collegial relationship. Over the years, we've continued our studies independently, and occasionally our paths crossed and we had an opportunity to work together. In the last decade, we've worked together in writing articles, sharing advice on research studies, and teaching classes. We have generally found that we shared many common thoughts and concerns about focus group interviewing.

During the 1990s, we found that interest in focus groups continued, and we both prepared second editions for our 1988 books. In 1995, the staff at Sage Publications asked us to consider developing a more in-depth treatment of focus group interviewing that would allow for more detail and guide researchers beyond the basic issues. We pondered the request and thought about how the materials might be presented. We weighed a variety of options and finally developed the kit in its present form. We developed this kit in an effort to help guide both novices and experts.

In these books, the authors have occasionally chosen to use the word *we*. Although the authors share many common experiences with focus groups, our approaches can and do vary, as we hope is the case with other researchers as well. When you see the word *we* in the books of this series, it typically refers to a judgment decision by the specific author(s) of that particular volume. Much of what the authors have learned about focus groups has been acquired, absorbed, and assimilated from the experiences of others. We use *we* in circumstances where one of us personally has experienced a situation that has been verified by another researcher or when a practice or behavior has become standard accepted practice by a body of focus group moderators. The use of *I,* on the other hand, tends to refer to situations and experiences that one of us has witnessed that may not have been verified by other researchers.

In terms of content, we decided on six volumes, each representing a separate theme. The volumes include the following:

- **Volume 1:** *The Focus Group Guidebook*

This volume provides a general introduction to focus group research. The central topics are the appropriate reasons for using focus groups and what you can expect to accomplish with them. This book is intended to help those who are new to focus groups.

- **Volume 2:** *Planning Focus Groups*

This volume covers the wide range of practical tasks that need to get done in the course of a research project using focus groups. A major topic is making the basic decisions about the group's format, such as the size of the groups, their composition, and the total number of groups.

- **Volume 3:** *Developing Questions for Focus Groups*

This book describes a practical process for identifying powerful themes and then offers an easy-to-understand strategy for translating those themes into questions. This book helps make the process of developing good questions doable by outlining a process and offering lots of examples.

- **Volume 4:** *Moderating Focus Groups*

The book is an overview of critical skills needed by moderators, the various approaches that successful moderators use, and strategies for handling difficult situations. Rookie moderators will find this book to be an invaluable guide, and veteran moderators will discover tips and strategies for honing their skills.

- **Volume 5:** *Involving Community Members in Focus Groups*

This book is intended for those who want to teach others to conduct focus group interviews, particularly nonresearchers in communities. Volunteers can often gather and present results more effectively than professionals. A critical element is how the volunteers are trained and the manner in which they work together.

- **Volume 6:** *Analyzing and Reporting Focus Group Results*

Analysis of focus group data is different from analysis of data collected through other qualitative methodologies, and this presents new challenges to researchers. This book offers an overview of important principles guiding focus group research and then suggests a systematic and verifiable analysis strategy.

Early on we struggled with how these materials might be presented. In order to help you find your way around the series, we developed several strategies. First, we are providing an expanded table of contents and an overview of topics at the beginning of each chapter. These elements help the reader quickly grasp the overall picture and understand the relationship between specific sections. Second, we've attempted to make the indexes as useful as possible. Volumes 2-6 contain two indexes: an index for that volume and a series index to help you find your way around the entire kit of six books. Finally, we are using icons to identify materials of interest. These icons serve several purposes. Some icons help you locate other materials within the series that amplify a particular topic. Other icons expand on a particular point, share a story or tip, or provide background material not included in the text. We like the icons because they have allowed us to expand on certain points without interrupting the flow of the discussion. The icons have also allowed us to incorporate the wisdom of other focus group experts. We hope you find them beneficial. We've also included icons in the book to help you discover points of interest.

The **BACKGROUND** icon identifies the bigger picture and places the current discussion into a broader context.

The **CAUTION** icon highlights an area where you should be careful. These are especially intended to help beginners spot potholes or potential roadblocks.

The **CHECKLIST** icon identifies a list of items that are good to think about; they may or may not be in a sequence.

The **EXAMPLE** icon highlights stories and illustrations of general principles.

The **EXERCISE** icon suggests something you could do to practice and improve your skills, or something you could suggest to others to help them improve their skills.

The **GO TO** icon is a reference to a specific place in this book or one of the other volumes where you will find additional discussion of the topic.

The **KEY POINT** icon identifies the most important things in each section. Readers should pay attention to these when skimming a section for the first time or reviewing it later.

The **TIP** icon highlights a good practice to follow or something that has worked successfully for us.

We hope you find this series helpful and interesting.

—Richard A. Krueger
St. Paul, Minnesota

—David L. Morgan
Portland, Oregon

About This Book

The intent of this book is to help researchers work with a team of volunteers in carrying out a focus group study. We're assuming that the volunteers have limited or no knowledge or experience with qualitative research. However, they do have other knowledge and skills that are essential to conducting the research. These volunteers have insights about the topic, experience working with people connected to the study, and an understanding of how the program, activity, or experience affects the lives of people. Furthermore, these volunteers are typically trusted and found to be credible to the target audience.

This book can also be used by instructors who wish to teach focus group interviewing skills to students. To us, the difference between students and a team of volunteers is subtle but significant. The difference lies in the goal of the instructor. In the teaching mode, the goal of the instructor is to build the skills and knowledge of the students. In the volunteer mode, the instructor's goal includes not only building skills and knowledge but also sharing decisions, giving away responsibilities, trusting decisions of volunteers, and respecting volunteers' experience.

We're concerned about the misuse of the term *focus group*. Over the past two decades, this term has attracted lots of attention and has been badly abused. Indeed, some criticism of "focus groups" is justified, because what have been called "focus groups" are often no such thing. Many of these bogus focus groups are conducted in community environments and, unfortunately, often with organizations that have precious few resources. These bogus groups regularly have one or more of the following characteristics:

- Moderators with no training or understanding of their role
- Groups with erratic attendance—too many or too few people attend
- Too few focus groups
- Groups with open invitations for the general public
- Groups that are perceived as threatening by participants
- Groups that have conflicting purposes (e.g., to convey the impression of openness or listening, when there is no intention on using results)
- Various group strategies mixed with no understanding of what each does (nominal groups, brainstorming, delphi technique, hearings, etc.)

For additional discussion of the characteristics of focus groups, look over the first volume of this series, *The Focus Group Guidebook.*

This book is divided into three sections. Chapter 1 provides background and grounding for working with others in research efforts. Chapter 2 offers a set of strategies that we've found helpful in team-based focus group studies. Chapter 3 includes examples of exercises to prepare a team of volunteers.

Caution:
Read This First

Throughout this book, we assume that you have had experience conducting focus group interviews. You must have conducted focus groups yourself before you can involve community members.

Based on our experience, there are three levels in teaching focus group interviewing. The first level is teaching about focus groups. This is the level often found in academic environments, such as in university research or methods courses. In these courses, the instructor has a general knowledge of focus groups and conveys the essential facts to students.

The second level is preparing individuals to conduct focus groups. This level requires the teacher to have experience in planning, conducting, and analyzing focus groups in order to demonstrate needed skills and to answer questions.

The third level is guiding a research team of nonresearchers in using focus groups. We feel that this level of instruction demands experience both in conducting focus group interviews and in working with groups. This book is intended for these second and third levels, and throughout this book, we assume that you've had this experience. At the third level, you find yourself leading a team in conducting focus groups. In this environment, you take on roles beyond that of the instructor. You become an adviser, planner, logistics coordinator, counselor, cheerleader, and more. Your challenge is to guide a team that has little or no background in focus groups in a research effort. The skills and background you need for this are different from merely telling about focus groups.

The differences among these levels are similar to the differences between teaching music appreciation, teaching individuals to play instruments, and conducting an orchestra. This is a book about conducting the orchestra.

If you lack skills in focus groups, consider putting yourself through a crash course. Begin by reading about focus groups. This kit is a sound beginning, but look over other sources as well. Participate in focus groups, or observe others conducting focus groups. Consider attending a class on conducting focus groups. Finally, conduct several focus groups yourself. Do the entire process yourself—designing the study, developing questions, recruiting participants, moderating the group, conducting the analysis, and, finally, reporting the results.

Get experience by volunteering to conduct a study for a community, social, athletic, or religious organization. Pick an organization where you've had some experience as a member, observer, or participant. Offer to conduct several focus groups to determine needs, develop strategies for improvement, or evaluate programs or services. Limit each group to about five or six participants, and plan for a one-hour discussion.

Once you've conducted several focus groups in an informal environment, plan and conduct several more groups in a more formal style. These next groups could include more participants (six to eight) and more questions (about a dozen), and could last longer (about two hours). Use the same focus group questions that you are asking others to use. This gives you an opportunity to pilot test the questions.

Get yourself a coach. Ask someone to help you conduct your focus group interviews. It is helpful to ask someone you trust, but even more desirable is to ask someone who is knowledgeable and familiar with moderating focus groups. A veteran moderator is ideal—but often hard to locate. Ask your coach to critique you. The coach might use the criteria for rating moderators in ICON F5. If a coach is not available, videotape yourself moderating the focus group. Note the description of this exercise in Chapter 3, Section F.

Prepare a summary report when you've finished conducting each group. This report can be used later as an example of what you want volunteers to prepare. Reflect on what you did particularly well and what you would do differently. Force yourself to write these observations down.

OK, now that you are grounded in the fundamentals of focus group interviewing, consider your grounding in people skills. For the team effort to be successful, the researcher will be expected to behave in a way that is unusual in the field of research, involving such activities as coaching, cheerleading, and mentoring. As researchers, we are taught to exercise control over a situation to enable precise measurement and ensure consistent conditions. Lack of control in research is seen by some as right up there with chaos, contamination, and disaster. In fact, when working with a team of volunteers, ambiguity, confusion, and perhaps even chaos will become the sine qua non. So, get ready to take on a role in which you no longer have complete control. If you aren't comfortable with your people skills, lead jointly with a person who exudes them. Look over Figure 1.1 in Chapter 1, where we illustrate differing levels of control for professionals and participants. As you move to the right (toward increased participant control), you also increase the probability of ambiguity.

At times, this lack of control will be vexing to you, the researcher. Team members will agonize over critical parts of the study, such as question development and audience selection. Sometimes you will think, "This would go so much faster if I just did it myself!" You will occasionally feel that you know a better way to frame the questions or structure the study. If so, you must put forth your positions clearly and coherently for the team to consider. The black box of research procedures no longer exists. It is essential that you are able to articulate research principles in commonsense, lay language. At the same time, you must be open to and respectful of the field wisdom of team members. Focus group studies are not precise formulas that are followed rigidly but rather human, social experiences. As a result, all factors that serve as incentives or barriers to that social communication are pertinent to the study, and this, then, is the territory where lay team members have unique expertise.

Attitude is a critical component. Each volunteer must be approached in an honoring, respectful manner. Each volunteer brings something to the study. Every person on the team has talents or insights that are so important that the team will suffer if that person does not fully contribute. Each difference is valuable. Every point of view or conflicting value is a strength. The team is diverse, but on one critical point the members are in complete agreement—the need for information derived from focus group interviews. This view must not only be believed but be articulated to the team by you, the researcher.

Finally, there is an additional researcher skill that is often overlooked: patience. Many times, you will feel that the process is going too slowly, and you may become frustrated with the lack of closure, the reopening of old arguments, and the lack of consensus—all of which are characteristics of team efforts. You are guiding a convoy that moves at the speed of the slowest vehicle. Some volunteers will be like snappy sports cars, able to turn on a dime, and others will be like lumbering semi-trailer trucks, with enormous inertia and great difficulty in changing directions. Your performance indicator is not the speed of the convoy but, rather, of the participation of all the individual vehicles.

Directory of Icons in Chapter 3

This is a directory of the icons used in Chapter 3. We hope that instructors will use these exercises, tips, and examples. To increase usefulness, we've developed a coding system to identify and catalog the icons that appear in this chapter.

A. LOCATING FOCUS GROUP PARTICIPANTS

B. RECRUITING FOCUS GROUP PARTICIPANTS

J. ANALYSIS AND REPORT WRITING

K. ORAL REPORTING

1

Background and Grounding

The Emergence of Participatory Studies

Overview

The Continuum of Volunteer Participation
The Evolution of Participatory Research Approaches
The Case for Volunteer Participation
When to Use "Professional" Researchers
When to Involve Volunteers in the Research Process
Countering the Naysayers
Summary

Collaborative evaluation, participatory evaluation, action research, community-initiated research, developmental evaluation, empowerment evaluation, organizational learning, continuous quality improvement—phrase after phrase naming inquiry processes involving volunteers. Whether or not you know what these processes involve, the mere fact that there are so many different names for them points to how common they are as we approach the next century. But why collaborative approaches, and why now? For people preparing to engage in focus group research, understanding the answers to these questions can mark an important beginning. The purpose of Chapter 1 is to give you background in the historical development of and conceptual rationale for volunteer participation.

The Continuum of Volunteer Participation

One way to think about volunteer participation in research is depicted in Figure 1.1. At one end of this continuum, outside experts—professional researchers or evaluators—direct and control the research process. They decide on the questions and methodology, collect and analyze the data, and then report back to their clients, who, in most cases, are somehow involved in the program being studied. In any good study, program administrators and staff necessarily take part; they provide information about the context, raise important issues for examination, give data, and so forth. But the responsibility for conducting the study remains in the hands of the professionals, as does the bulk of the actual work involved. This is the traditional approach to program evaluation that developed in the 1960s.

The opposite end of the continuum documents a dramatically different approach to the inquiry process; at this extreme, program staff and participants study themselves with minimal involvement from professional researchers. They formalize issues for study, develop surveys, collect information, and then reflect on its meaning for their program. For those formally trained in the methods of social science, this is an impossible venture. Depending on their orientation to the research process, they may well ask, with varying degrees of concern, "How can untrained novices do valid research?" What these professionals may not realize, however, is that good practitioners have always conducted a form of practical inquiry, asking questions about their work and looking for information to document success or to decide on needed change. In some cases, ordinary citizens who are not program staff conduct studies to help them make sense of their world. Such research may not adhere strictly to the canons of quantitative or qualitative science, but it is sensible inquiry with a specific purpose: to understand what works in a given context.

Many people—researchers and practitioners alike—are reluctant to work at the practitioner extreme of the continuum. However, participatory approaches at the mid-range of the continuum, involving varying degrees of control by professional researchers, can increase the roles played by volunteers in the research process. For a number of reasons, people are increasingly choosing such approaches. The important points to remember are that the continuum does exist and that volunteers today can rightfully take ownership of and play key roles in studying their own programs. A brief summary of the history of the field suggests that this has not always been the case.

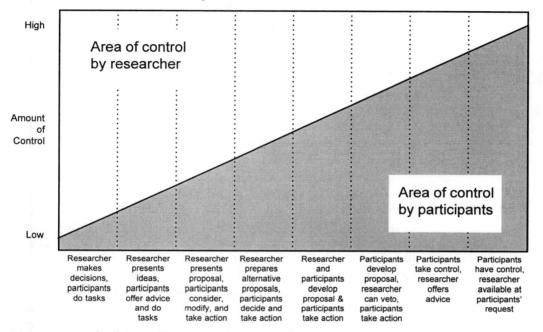

Figure 1.1   Levels of Control Between Researchers and Participants

The Evolution of Participatory Research Approaches

When program evaluation emerged as a field in the 1960s, it borrowed its methodology in large part from the methods of quantitative research. This was no surprise. Many of those hired to conduct large-scale evaluation studies worked in research universities where such approaches predominated. These were the methods of "science" that, in the minds of many, could generate truth about the programs being studied. The stereotypical role of the researchers applying these methods required that they remain neutral, "objective," removed from the fray. They applied special skills in a systematic and careful manner, seeking to avoid contamination from the site being studied. To these stereotypical researchers, it would be unthinkable for lay people to help with the research effort. Volunteers would necessarily spoil the study. They would get in the way, contaminate the variables, and waste everyone's time. Their participation in research would be akin to asking someone off the street to join a medical team for open-heart surgery. If you were a patient, you might well be troubled by this approach.

As the field developed, however, concern arose that evaluation results were not always useful to the individuals who had commissioned studies, truth or no truth. The stakeholder approach to evaluation emerged in the 1970s as a solution to this problem. Involving stakeholders, meaning all those who had a stake in a program, helped ensure that studies would take on issues of importance to those involved. Robert Stake's notion of responsive evaluation and, later, Michael Quinn Patton's framing of utilization-focused evaluation highlighted the central role that stakeholders should play if evaluation results were to prove useful.

Naturalistic methodology was a related development, emerging as a technique for addressing certain types of evaluation questions. This approach began with a different set of assumptions from the more traditional research paradigm. Evaluators using a qualitative approach could not assume that they knew best but instead would elicit wisdom and grounding from local people during a study. Issues and questions might well change during the course of the research, and, as information unfolded, it could influence the study. These assumptions reflect a different understanding of the world and dramatically affect the research process. At professional conferences, partisans of two traditions—the quantitative paradigm and its qualitative counterpart—argued contentiously about an appropriate place for each. At the same time, the evaluation field listened as proponents of total quality management, also known as continuous quality improvement, pointed to the bottom-line improvements possible when companies implemented a participatory, data-based change process.

Over two decades, then, evaluators came to realize the potential value of asking others for help, given the collaborative nature of their work. People involved in programs being studied—policymakers, staff members, clients, and, in some cases, even the general public—could play valuable roles in the evaluation process. These roles could be fairly limited (e.g., raising issues and framing questions); alternatively, practitioners could become extremely active in the actual process of the evaluation itself.

In the 1990s, several forms of participatory evaluation have emerged. Michael Quinn Patton's notion of developmental evaluation couples an evaluator with professional staff early in the development of a program so that evaluation information can help make sense of the growth process. Cousins and Earl (1995) define their own version of participatory evaluation through which professional researchers teach evaluation processes to practitioners over time. Action research in both traditional and practitioner-centered forms has become the topic of numerous articles (King and Lonnquist, 1992), and David Fetterman uses the phrase *empowerment evaluation* to describe a form of inquiry that seeks to empower directly those who participate. Having moved beyond the time when professional researchers alone controlled evaluation studies, there is now no shortage of participatory approaches for actively involving volunteers. `

The Case for Volunteer Participation

Regardless of how widespread participatory approaches are, some may still question the benefits of volunteer participation in research studies. On the one hand, the risks of handing over a technical process to people unfamiliar with its complexity are easily imagined. What if volunteers don't recruit an appropriate sample? What if they ask leading interview questions, or what if they aren't able to capture or record the subtleties of what is said? What will prevent them from finding support for only their own opinions? On the other hand, a strong rationale underlies the inclusion of volunteer participants in key roles in focus group studies. The rationale has practical, historical, and psychological components.

There are four practical reasons for volunteer participation in focus group studies.

First, in many situations, an outside researcher may be unlikely, or even unable, to collect the in-depth, inside data that a community member volunteer can elicit. People often feel more comfortable sharing their real thoughts and opinions with a person they know or with someone whose background is similar to theirs. Byrd Baylor (1993) describes an extreme example of this phenomenon in *Yes Is Better Than No,* when a naive researcher, having put on a Navaho belt buckle and blue jeans, assumes that he is gathering good data from a group of native people at a local bar. In fact, the bemused Indians are only too aware of his naïveté, emphasized by his superficial effort to blend in, and they proceed to give him answers that he seems to want, rather than their own thoughts on the issues raised. Using local volunteers to gather meaningful information could perhaps have solved his problem and saved his study. What is particularly worrisome in the example is that the researcher is unaware of what has happened and assumes that the data gathered are actually worth using.

Second, a highly pragmatic reason for using volunteers is that they increase the feasibility of conducting studies in settings where a more traditional research design would be prohibitively expensive and simply out of the question. Because they will work for free or with minimal support, volunteers are extremely cost-effective. Volunteers can work creatively with professional researchers to ensure the quality of a study while keeping costs down. For example, if a researcher develops questions and organizes the evaluation, trained volunteers may be able to collect sizable amounts of data and, under supervision, analyze the results. The key is to use the professional evaluator to design appropriately rigorous processes and to maintain a focus on quality control.

Third, one of the presumed benefits of volunteers' participation in studies is the increased likelihood that they will care about the results. The assumption is that if people are actively involved during a study—framing questions, collecting data, helping to analyze results—they will want to apply what they have learned during the process. In other words, they will use the evaluation results, which, for many evaluators, remains a primary reason for conducting any study and the hallmark of a good one. A related benefit may be volunteers' increased awareness of the evaluation process per se and their ability over time to participate in increasingly sophisticated ways. Some organizations are now encouraging staff and volunteers to conduct their own studies—in other words, working at the practitioner extreme of the research control continuum. The highly touted notion of organizational learning suggests the possibility that entire organizations can eventually become knowledgeable about their own processes and products, actively integrating data-based changes into ongoing functions.

Fourth, those who participate as volunteers may benefit as individuals, and these benefits may help strengthen the organizations in which they work. People who have learned research skills as volunteers often discuss personal benefits, such as new skills or increased self-confidence. Many times, they report having fun being a part of what they believe to be an important process and getting to know other volunteers in a special way. It is hard to describe the exhilaration present during a discussion of data that documents exactly what people expected or, by contrast, surprises the volunteers who collected the information. Some people may become committed to acting on something they have learned. And, because the participation relates to research, some individuals even report increased empowerment, either as a person or as an organization, because they see how to collect information about what is happening in their setting and realize that they can do this over time. This is no small by-product of the volunteer process.

These are the practical reasons for using volunteers. There are other, more conceptual reasons as well. The historical component of the rationale for volunteer participation relates directly to the Progressive movement that the United States experienced early in the 20th century. This widespread movement divided roughly into two types of reforms: conservative, which was concerned with social order and the application of scientific expertise; and liberal, which stressed social justice and increased citizen participation.

These distinctions parallel similar divisions in the field of program evaluation today. Traditional approaches are more conservative, using "scientific" processes to study what is happening in programs and giving the role of expert to those with research skills. By contrast, participatory approaches, which welcome and encourage volunteer participation, have descended from liberal Progressives like John Dewey. These approaches seek to reform programs—and, eventually, perhaps even society—through increased citizen participation in evaluation processes. The idea is that if people take an active part in studying programs and organizations, their perspectives will become part of an ongoing development, adding a richness that is missing from traditional evaluation approaches and giving voice to those previously unheard. The historical reason for including volunteers as active par- ticipants in studies, then, is that in doing so, we may ultimately move toward a more just society, one where the ideas of all are included in discussion and one that values people's participation. Even if society is slow to change, volunteers' active involvement in the interim renews the vision of Progressive reformers who sought to increase people's participation in activities affecting their lives.

A final reason for using volunteers in studies comes from psychological principles. Recent developments in constructivist theory point to the powerful learning that can occur if people are engaged in a process that creates or "constructs" knowledge. Studying a program or an organization is a different kind of involvement for most people, and volunteers working on an evaluation can come to know their settings in rich and interesting ways. By facilitating focus groups and other forms of data collection, they are encouraged to think differently about what they are doing. Long-held ideas, assumptions, and misconceptions may be reinforced or challenged. Evaluation questions may evolve, and new questions may arise. If you want people to understand a program or context, have them serve as volunteers on a research project. The resultant learning can be well worth the effort.

In summary, when making the case for volunteer participation, you can point to three kinds of potential benefits.

- Individual volunteers may benefit, feeling more knowledgeable about both the program they study and evaluation methods more generally. This may increase their commitment to making realistic and appropriate changes to strengthen their program in the future, and it can open their eyes to other research possibilities.

- Programs and organizations may benefit through cost-effective studies that yield usable information on issues that matter, because they tap into volunteers who are interested in putting the results to use.
- Some may argue that society as a whole may benefit to the extent that volunteer participation increases democratic processes, and, although this can be extremely difficult to document, this argument may appeal to the idealistic among us.

The various components of the rationale for including volunteers in research activities—practical, historical, and psychological— suggest numerous reasons for doing so. And, for those who believe that using volunteers unavoidably and by definition challenges the rigor and credibility of the research process, there is one more answer: Technical accuracy is only one of the categories of standards contained in the publication of the Joint Committee on Standards for Educational Program Evaluation (1994). What participatory approaches may give up in accuracy is more than balanced by what they gain in two other categories: feasibility and utility. Therein lies the value of using volunteers.

KEY POINT

What Participatory Approaches Give Up in Accuracy Is More Than Balanced by What They Gain in Feasibility and Utility

When to Use "Professional" Researchers

Although a strong case exists for the use of volunteers, it is not always proper or even advisable to involve them. It is important to know when and how to use professional researchers, that is, people who earn their living conducting research and evaluation studies. They have been formally trained in research methods of one type or another and typically hold master's or doctoral degrees. In some cases, hiring such professionals is not only appropriate but essential to the eventual success of a project. This would be true in the following situations:

- The required research is complex or demands technical skills. One of the reasons that researchers are able to support themselves professionally is that they possess technical knowledge and a set of specialized skills that other people lack. Research is not like changing a lightbulb. Not everyone knows the specifics of multiple regression or qualitative analysis, and it is often necessary to pay someone for such work. It is also worth paying a researcher to organize and coordinate a complicated study that involves multiple sites or sizable numbers of interviews.

- You need the perspective of an outsider. Some situations are so complicated to those who are living them that the eyes of an objective outsider can become extremely useful. The distance and questions of a newcomer may help to clarify what is taking place.
- You have funding to support a study. People who run programs and businesses may not have the time or desire to conduct research on their practice. If money is available for someone else to conduct a study, it may be the best option simply to do so.
- The product of the research is more important than its process. Researchers have recently come to understand that, in some cases, the process of engaging in a study is as important—if not more important—than the actual outcome of the research. But this is not always the case. In some situations, what is needed are data to complete a bureaucratic form or a formal report to send to someone for accountability purposes. In such cases, hiring a professional researcher to take care of the task takes one item off of a "to do" list.
- The program or situation to be studied is highly political. We would argue that every program ever created has brought politics to life, but in those cases where political challenges hold the potential to damage the research process, the credentials and knowledge of someone from outside may have a neutralizing effect. There are surely no guarantees, but the distance an outside researcher can rightly bring to a study may be essential both to its eventual successful conclusion and to the acceptance of its results.

When to Involve Volunteers in the Research Process

You can identify those situations where volunteers might participate actively in the research process by simply reversing the situations where it's appropriate to use "professional" researchers. In these cases, the meaningful participation of program volunteers not only makes sense but can take advantage of the special skills that they bring to studying their programs and contexts. Such situations include the following:

- The required research is not complex or does not demand highly technical skills. Many times, the research that projects or programs need is fairly straightforward, especially if the programs are relatively small in size. In such cases, the strict notion of "scientific rigor" can appropriately give way to a localized approach that creates information for people to apply in their own setting. Volunteers are able to collect such information if they focus on using methods that are sufficiently rigorous.

- You need the knowledge and perspective of insiders. Some situations are so complicated that an objective outsider unfamiliar with the context may be unable to understand the complexity of events or the subtle nuances present in people's actions. The active involvement and direct participation of individuals connected with a program may help make sense of what is taking place, not just as a source of data but also in framing the study and in collecting and analyzing information.

- You don't have funding to support a study. Numerous projects, programs, and agencies lack sufficient (or, in some cases, any) funding to conduct research and evaluation. Research can be seen as a luxury in times of budget cuts when program staff must choose between direct service to clients or a research effort. In the absence of funding, volunteers can provide essential person-power for organizing and completing a cost-effective study.

- The process of the research is more important than its product. In many settings, the activities associated with a research study can encourage or even require people to think in new ways about what they are doing. Together they collect and make sense of data about their situation, and this process can be a powerful force for change in an organization. Michael Quinn Patton labels this "process use"—the use of the research or evaluation process itself, rather than the use of any product generated.

- The program or situation to be studied is not highly political. Although we would argue that, by definition, every research situation is political, not all are highly politicized. In those cases where people can realistically come together around an inquiry process that has the potential for positive outcomes, volunteers may well be important contributors to the research effort.

Countering the Naysayers

Warning: Using volunteers in a study may be harmful to your mental health. You may well be criticized because many people are either unaware of the continuum shown in Figure 1.1 or cannot accept any movement toward the practitioner end. It is disquieting, to say the least, if people attack you because you have assigned a sizable role in your study to volunteers. Listed below, then, are several common criticisms of participatory approaches, along with potential responses to them.

- *It's bad research if volunteers participate.* One common criticism is a blanket condemnation of all participatory approaches—in other words, the statement that if volunteers participate, the focus group research is bad by definition. Some people simply can't accept a role for individuals who have not been formally trained in research methods at a university, fearing the potential damage that a careless or poorly designed study might cause. The case for volunteer participation given above was written with these individuals in mind, and you need to help them understand how the field has changed in the past two decades. Like it or not, people without formal research credentials are now participating in studies, and there are many situations where volunteers can offer both time and important insights. Providing examples of successful studies that volunteers have conducted may be helpful, as can more theoretical articles that make the case for this process. However, what is at stake here is a value commitment, and the question often boils down to this: Is it better to do no study at all or to have volunteers participate in the best study possible under the circumstances? Some people may opt for the former and decide not to proceed with a study. That choice may, in fact, be preferable as it is better not to start than to start with only a halfhearted commitment to the process.

- *Volunteers are not qualified to conduct focus group research.* Sadly, there is evidence to support this criticism. Many well-intentioned people have conducted what they called "focus groups," where, to cite one example, the moderator kept interrupting people and explaining his answer—presumably the correct one—to the questions. Very quickly, those around the table stopped speaking, and he proceeded with his monologue. Many of us have taken part in studies like this, studies that were, to put it kindly, less than adequate. However, you can appropriately respond in three ways.

  — First, you can explain the training process that volunteers have gone through prior to conducting the study. The techniques described in this book will teach people the technical skills of focus group research, and, as long as volunteers apply what they have learned and monitor their process, they are qualified for the work.

— Second, if your study has a professional consultant conducting the training and monitoring the process, you can refer critics to that individual's commitment to and acceptance of participation.

— Third, you can build on the important claim that, although they may not be professional researchers, volunteers are active members of the group being studied, and because of this, they have insider knowledge that may be invaluable to the process. Focus group participants may be more willing to tell volunteers than outsiders what they think, regardless of the experts' formal credentials.

- *It's inefficient to train volunteers to do what research professionals do.* Even people who accept the general idea of volunteer participation may question whether or not it's worthwhile to spend valuable time teaching people skills that they may use only once in their lives. But inefficiency is not always bad. As Mae West once put it, "Anything worth doing is worth doing slowly." We suggest three responses to this criticism.

— First, the potential benefits of teaching volunteers research skills may outweigh the inefficiency of doing so. As discussed above, these benefits may affect individuals directly as they learn specific skills and information or feel empowered to take action. They may also affect the organization as a whole in two ways: by fostering a commitment to use the information gathered; and by simultaneously creating the capacity to engage in additional research.

— Second, by training volunteers and encouraging them to participate in a research process, you have demonstrated your commitment to a democratic form of research, one that values a variety of people's perspectives and holds the expectation that what is learned will make a difference. Democracy is simply not efficient, but for centuries its value has been upheld.

— Third, inefficient or not, volunteer participation is usually much cheaper than hiring someone to do the entire study. Given the choice, many people might not wallpaper their bedroom, paint their house, or cater their wedding by themselves, but that is sometimes the most cost-effective option.

Summary

Chapter 1 has presented a conceptual background and grounding for involving volunteers in focus group research. As Figure 1.1 suggests, there is a range of possibilities for participation, and in the past two decades, researchers in applied settings have increasingly requested assistance from people who lack formal research training but who have direct experience in programs or organizations, whether they provide or receive service. The rationale for volunteer participation rests on the simple claim that when people are involved in studies, good things happen. They may more easily tap into information from their peers and colleagues. They are often willing to work without fees. Because they care about the information that they collect, they may see that it gets used. Through taking part, they may also benefit individually from learning firsthand about research.

Volunteers, however, are not always the solution to every research problem. If you decide to recruit them, make sure that the situation is one that will benefit from their participation. Plan in advance your response to potential criticisms, and make sure that you personally feel comfortable with the approach. In Chapter 2, you will find a set of strategies that we have used for team-based focus group studies. These will assist you in designing and managing volunteer involvement.

2

How to Involve Volunteers

In this chapter, we will introduce the concept of collaborative focus groups, describe the critical players, offer suggestions on how to make collaboration successful, suggest a training curriculum, and then present an example of a training plan.

Collaborative Focus Groups

For the past several decades, if you wanted to conduct focus groups and didn't have the expertise, the only option available was to hire an outside expert. The outside expert would conduct the research, present the report, and move on. There are many advantages to using these outside researchers, and this book is not intended to diminish the importance of their role and contributions. Indeed, it is because experts have made focus groups look so easy that others have been tempted to try them. Complex endeavors, whether in sports, music, or focus groups, look effortless when performed by a master.

More recently, a variety of organizations have used other options to conduct focus groups. One option was to assign a staff member who knew how to conduct focus groups to carry out the study. This offered advantages in terms of lowering research costs and building employee skills. A second advantage was that other employees observed, became interested, and sought to develop their skills as well. This led to another option, which included a research team. The research team comprised a variety of people, some of whom were familiar with research and some of whom possessed other forms of knowledge and expertise. Not only did these studies produce credible results, but they also yielded unanticipated side effects: enhanced credibility for the study, a commitment to the recommendations, and a sense of empowerment among participants. Studies were more powerful if volunteers were actively involved in framing the problem, gathering the information, preparing the report, and sharing the findings.

We have learned that if staff and outside groups are expected to support and promote alternative policies and procedures, then it is wise to involve them early and in meaningful ways. This involvement needs to go beyond a briefing meeting or a colorful flyer describing the most recent management decisions.

The model that has evolved has been a collaborative approach that places volunteers, staff members, and nonresearchers at the center of the focus group project. They are charged with conducting the study. These individuals are often carefully recruited and possess certain talents and resources that can contribute to overall success.

Here are some examples of collaborative studies.

State Department of Education

Bonnie was an employee of a State Department of Education. She was given the task of conducting a needs assessment of children with emotional and behavioral disorders. The end product would potentially change legislation affecting these children. Early on in the project, Bonnie began to consider focus groups because she wanted parents and youth, as well as a variety of caregivers, to share their experiences, identify needs, and profit from the comments of others. The budget demands of a sizable study caused Bonnie to hesitate about hiring a research agency. Bonnie was skillful in getting people together and had unique talents in persuading individuals of various backgrounds to lend a hand. She already had a task force committed to the study and had contacts with target audiences. She did hire an outside expert— but not to conduct the focus groups. The expert trained the task force to conduct the focus groups throughout the state. When the report was completed, the task force used the report, which was based on their collective experiences, to formulate recommendations for action. The task force members went back to their communities and continued to push for the adoption of the recommendations. Not only were the recommendations adopted, but legislation was enacted based on the study and the task force's work.

A Community Assessment Effort

In the early 1990s, a national program encouraged local organizations to work together to prevent drug and alcohol use by young people. One such program began in Dakota County, Minnesota. Dakota County, within the Twin Cities metropolitan area, includes urban, suburban, and rural communities. The national program encouraged the formation of coalitions, and in this county, the coalition was called the Dakota Alliance for Prevention (DAP). Early on, DAP leaders wanted to conduct a qualitative needs assessment that would complement the statistical data already available on drug and alcohol use among young people. The advisory board and staff of DAP initiated a focus group study whereby a team of teens and parents was trained to conduct focus groups with others in the community. The teens and parents were selected to reflect the geographic and cultural diversity of the county. The volunteers were good sports, willing to offer their time and talents to a task that was unfamiliar. As the training proceeded, the team became more interested, but the members were still doubtful about the possibility of making real changes. When the training was completed and the team was about to begin the study, one volunteer said, "We're willing to help with this effort because it's interesting, but I really doubt that we can make a difference on teen use of alcohol and drugs. The problem is just too big and too complex."

Team members conducted focus groups and reassembled to share their results. The sharing was energizing as teens and parents described their findings and offered solution strategies that were suggested by the focus group participants. Several themes were evident, and the research team members began to gain confidence that they could make a difference. Some members of the task force even went to local boards and media to offer suggestions on workable strategies that both teens and parents could use.

In this study, focus groups provided information on a community concern, but of greater value was the feeling of hope that it provided to a team of volunteers. The members of the team now understood the problem in a way that statistical data could not offer. They witnessed teens and parents agonizing over the problem and wanting to make changes. Changes were made because a team now owned the problem and understood how members of the community could work together.

The University Listens

The Minnesota Extension Service is one of the primary outreach units of the University of Minnesota. Through its network of more than 80 field offices and more than 300 extension educators, the organization provides educational programs on topics that range from farming to home horticulture, from family economics to youth development, from helping local businesses to assisting large-scale community economic development. Because the Minnesota Extension Service had broadened to many new audiences over the previous decade, administrators requested a study that would seek out customer opinions on this diversity of programs.

A collaborative focus group project began with a diverse study team. The team of 25 included employees (field staff, university specialists, clerical and support staff), as well as those affected by extension outreach programs (mayors, county commissioners, representatives of local and state agencies). Each member of the team was matched with a partner with a different background and assigned to conduct several groups. After conducting a series of focus groups with employees, customer groups, and partner agencies, the research team reconvened to share results. The results highlighted the lack of a consistent and uniform image of the organization—among both customers and employees. While these and other results were beneficial, so were the side benefits. Those who participated in the focus group discussions indicated their appreciation that someone had listened to them. Too often, employees, partners, and customers felt they were told answers, solutions, and approaches, rather than being asked for their input. The listening process was an indication of a caring organization. Another benefit was the enhanced listening skills of each study team member. After this successful experience, a number of the team members conducted focus groups on other topics.

Customer Service

Federal agencies of the U.S. government have recently been required to document how they listen and respond to customers. The U.S. Department of Agriculture wanted not only to listen to customers but also to find out how to develop a complaint system that met customer concerns. To conduct the study, a research team was assembled that consisted of employees from differing subunits and geographic locations. The team members worked in pairs and conducted more than 30 focus groups in 18 states. Armed with the results, USDA policymakers were able to identify improved strategies for being responsive to customer needs and to develop an improved complaint system.

The team approach enhanced internal credibility for the study and helped the entire research team to work together across agency lines on areas of common concern. Another side benefit was the favorable response from many customers who appreciated the chance to express their concerns, face-to-face, with someone representing the USDA.

The collaborative approach to focus group research includes community members on the research team. The community may be a geographic community, a community of employees, a community of color, or any other group representing a characteristic by which people identify themselves. The benefit of the collaborative approach is that those community members

- add credibility to the study,
- help ensure that the study addresses concerns as seen by members of the community (relevance), and
- add to the likelihood of use because community members often know what's needed to implement recommendations.

KEY POINT

Involving the Community Adds Credibility, Ensures Relevance, Increases Use

The collaborative approach introduces complexity but also yields additional benefits. With the collaborative approach, new features are now included. The study goes beyond the mere discovery of information and includes

- developing skills among the participants,
- creating awareness among influential individuals by having them involved in the study, and
- generating support for viable solutions.

The process of gathering data and listening takes on more importance. In many studies, this process is as valuable as the study findings are.

John McKnight from Northwestern University has spent years studying communities and the connection between communities and universities. McKnight contends that one difficulty is in the communication between communities and institutions of higher education. Universities do not understand the knowledge and belief system of communities. University researchers assume that the rest of the world believes, understands, and processes information in the same way as researchers do. Because university researchers get their cutting-edge information from research studies in professional meetings and journals, they assume that others have the same process for finding credible information. In fact, people in communities have less belief in studies and more belief in stories. What is persuasive to local residents is that information be told to them by a credible and trusted person. The information often comes in the form of a story. Perhaps this is why collaborative focus groups have such persuasive appeal. The stories that emerge from focus groups are credible to communities, and the resulting study is also believable to the researcher.

What Do We Mean by "Volunteer"?

A volunteer is . . .

- a colleague who offers to help,
- the outfielder from your softball team who's willing to lend a hand,
- the teenager with the squeaky voice who lives down the block and wants experience,
- the senior citizen across the street who's interested in helping people,
- a graduate student who wants something to put on his resumé,
- the advocate who wants a better future for her child.

They may be motivated by different things, but a volunteer is anyone who is willing to offer time, talent, and energy to accomplish a task.

Let's think about the types of people who might be involved in a focus group research project. We will be using four names to describe differing types of people who may be assisting in the activity. These names are *volunteer, student, researcher,* and *research team.* Let's look at these roles in more depth.

A *volunteer* is an individual who has agreed to assist with the study. We're using the term *volunteer* to include all members of a research team, except the researchers but including paid staff members, who in fact may be authorized or even assigned to the study team. It also includes lay people, members of advisory boards, employees, officers of associations, elected officials, students, and a host of other people. These volunteers are brought together by an interest in the study, and they all have made some commitment to help gather information. They may not agree with each other about past solution strategies or policies, and, indeed, they may even have wide-ranging opinions on the nature of the problem. However, they are committed to gather information about the topic and to do so in an open, honest, and respectful manner. All volunteers have committed themselves to investing some time in this effort.

Volunteers possess skills and valuable background knowledge. This knowledge may be related to the topic, the organizational history, the people you wish to listen to, the policies and rules relating to the problem, or a host of other factors. This background enriches the study because it allows data to be seen through a host of different filters. As the diversity of the research team increases, the potential for workable solution strategies increases as well, but so does the time investment in conducting the study.

Student is the term we use to identify people seeking to learn about focus group interviewing. Students are usually expected to carry out instructions and to follow the lead of others. Ordinarily, the wisdom and past experiences of students are not valued, at least not like those of volunteers. Students are typically found in structured classrooms with exams, standard hours of instruction and specific directions. The primary objective is to learn knowledge and skills. By contrast, the primary goal of volunteers is to accomplish a task.

There is a major difference between students and volunteers. (Here we are referring to formal classes where students learn focus group skills. We acknowledge that students can also be volunteers.) Both may be seekers of information, and both can gain from the experiences suggested in this section. Students, however, are subordinate to their teachers, while volunteers, by contrast, are equals. Volunteers can walk away at any time. They stay with you because they want to solve a problem, identify core needs, improve a program, revise rules and regulations, or accomplish whatever it was that brought about the study.

The *researcher* is the individual who provides leadership to a team of volunteers. The researcher is a teacher, coach, and mentor. This book is written for researchers, and we assume that you, as a researcher, have had previous experience with focus group interviewing and with qualitative research.

The *research team* is a group of people composed of the researcher and the team of volunteers who will assist with the study. We suggest that the size of the group be limited to foster effective communication, decision making, and progress toward goals. We've worked with teams ranging in size from a handful to 25 people. Clearly, it is more difficult to have a workable research team when the group size gets over a dozen people. When you do have more than a dozen people, you may want to select or elect a subgroup of people to become an advisory board that then makes the operational decisions relating to the study.

What Brings Volunteers Together?

So, what makes this group of people a team? Just calling them a research team is not enough. Experts who have studied teams have found that teams develop in a rather predictable manner. The process begins when a group of individuals is brought together. The challenge of leadership is to define clearly a common goal that becomes accepted and internalized by the group. Sometimes, this goal comes from authority figures, and other times, it emerges from the grassroots level. The goal may be complex or simple and straightforward. Whatever the source, there is a clear and understandable purpose that guides later behavior. The group typically goes through four stages, called *forming, storming, norming,* and *performing.*

Stage 1. Forming

The forming stage of team development is filled with uncertainty about the task, leadership, functions and responsibilities. There can be excitement about being together as well as lingering suspicions and anxiety about the task. When the individuals begin to think of themselves as part of a group, they are ready to move into the next stage.

Stage 2. Storming

In the second stage, participants begin to realize the difficulty of the task, and differences within the group become more visible. This stage is critical and is often the most difficult. People express concern about control and the process of moving ahead. This stage is completed when there is a clear sense of leadership and decision making within the group.

Stage 3. Norming

A sense of cohesiveness develops in this stage, and group rules (norms) are accepted and followed willingly. In the storming stage, the group sensed confusion, but in the norming stage, there is a feeling that all will work out in an acceptable manner. The group develops a sense of identity and is eager to take action.

Stage 4. Performing

Finally, the group is ready to perform. Roles are understood, leadership is clear, and decision-making patterns are established. Individuals work in concert, supporting and assisting each other in achieving goals.

For More Information on Team Development, see *The Team Handbook*, 1993, by Peter R. Scholtes et al.

In our experience with focus group teams, we've found the following principles to be helpful, and we offer them for your consideration:

Axioms for Focus Group Teams

- Be clear about the goal. *The purpose of the study will be the glue that holds the team together. The goal must be stated clearly and built on values held by the team.*
- Be patient. *Groups take time to work. Allow sufficient time for the group to get acquainted, relate to each other, listen to each other, and learn from each other. There is a delicate balance between being task driven and process driven. Too much emphasis on either dimension can erode commitment.*
- Create a climate of respect. *All views are respected, and all opinions are honored. The leaders state and demonstrate that there are no "wrong" answers, but only differing ways to see reality. The quest of the team is to find out how others see reality. There is a fundamental and critical difference between disagreement and lack of respect. Differing points of view are welcome and even encouraged. All views are respected, but while participants can be enthusiastic about a particular view, they must always be willing to "let the data speak" about differing realities.*
- Create a climate of learning. *The purpose of the exercise is to learn together about how an issue, policy, solution, strategy, or product is seen by targeted groups of people. The team will learn from the focus group participants and from each other.*
- Share leadership. *In these situations, several heads are better than one. Leadership can occur at several levels and is often shared by several individuals. For example, the researcher typically provides technical leadership, whereas another individual will provide the coordination of the team, logistics, timeline, and budget.*
- Be explicit. *We've found that people tend to take shortcuts on complex or time-consuming assignments. Sometimes, this is acceptable and even practical. Other times, it can jeopardize the study. As a result, we've learned the importance of being exceedingly explicit on the critical aspects of the study. For example, we are rigid when we describe systematic recruitment procedures, critical questions on the questioning route, note taking, or electronic recording.*

Should You Undertake a Collaborative Study?

Before deciding to use a collaborative approach, the researcher and study director should weigh the advantages and disadvantages of seeking help from others. Here is a checklist that may help you make the decision:

CHECKLIST

Is Collaborative Study for You?

☐ *Is this a study where volunteers are able to get information that is otherwise unavailable to researchers?*

☐ *Is this a study where volunteers can help stretch scarce resources? Calculate the costs of professionals versus volunteers.*

☐ *Is this a study where volunteers will increase the likelihood that the results will be used? Is this important to you?*

☐ *Is this a study where it is important for volunteers to develop new skills and self-confidence?*

☐ *Is this a study where it is important that volunteers learn more about the program?*

☐ *Do you have the time to work with a team of volunteers?*

☐ *Are you able to provide adequate training and supervision to volunteers?*

☐ *Will others believe that rigor was lost because of the use of multiple moderators or volunteers?*

☐ *Do you have a pool of talented volunteers from which to draw?*

☐ *Do researchers have the patience, perseverance, and skills to work with a team of nonresearchers in a respectful and honoring manner?*

The Collaborative Process

We offer you a process that has been helpful to a variety of organizations:

• Consider the alternatives. Before you proceed, consider the alternatives. Should you as the researcher do this study? Should you seek out another researcher to conduct the study? Should you seek out others to help you with the group process? Here are some of the factors that have guided our decision making.

Time: A collaborative process takes more time. If a normal focus group study would take 2 months, then a collaborative process would likely take 6 months. In fact, the larger the collaborative group, the longer the time needed to complete the study.

Cost: The cost of a collaborative study will depend on the time horizon of the study and if volunteer time is factored into the cost. One benefit of a collaborative process is the development of a talent pool of volunteers (or staff) who will be able to assist with future studies, making these future studies much more affordable. There are costs in training a cadre of volunteers, and if they are used only once, the research costs are high. Once these volunteers are trained and have experience, they become a valuable resource to the organization. Another cost concern is the degree to which volunteer time is factored into the study. If volunteers are salaried employees whose time is calculated into overall costs, then the price of the participation in research is steep. If, however, the time devoted to the study is considered as training or staff development, the research costs drop.

Talent: Certain talents are needed to conduct a collaborative study, such as recruiting, moderating, and analyzing. The researcher or someone on the team must possess skills in group process and team building.

Commitment to the study: Participants who are involved in planning the research, conducting the study, analyzing the results, and developing recommendations are far more likely to endorse and support the application of those recommendations. If a need for commitment is the driving force, this circumstance favors collaboration.

• **Prepare the plan.** This task occurs at the beginning of the study and is often completed by individuals or groups who control resources and determine policy. The task involves setting overall strategy and sanctioning the study (or, at least, approving preliminary consideration). Sometimes, those making this decision will want estimates of resources and brief plans of how the focus groups will operate, how people will be involved, and the expected outcomes. Here's an outline of what this plan might contain:

Project Proposal
    A. Name of the project
    B. Description of the problem, concern, or issue
    C. Background and past efforts
    D. Proposal for action (step-by-step)
    E. Participants
        – Research team
        – Volunteers
        – Focus group participants

F. Expected outcome
G. Possible risks, dangers, or limitations
H. Timeline
I. Budget

After the general plan has been approved by the funders, it needs to be fine-tuned by the research team. The vision of the overall strategy needs to be translated into specific action steps, and the research team must feel a sense of ownership in this process. Planning skills and research skills are both needed here to develop the specifics of the study, including determining the target population, the number and location of focus groups, and a refined estimate of needed resources. The researcher plays an important part in this task. The appendix at the end of this chapter includes a sample training plan.

• Recruit team members. When using volunteers or staff, one of the issues is the degree to which you can select the research team. Sometimes, you have no choice and need to use whomever is available. Other times, you may be able to make the selection. Give thought to the types of people you need. Here are some things we've learned in working with groups.

Pick Someone With Contacts

You'll likely need someone to help you make contacts with the target audience. This individual understands the target segment, may be a member of that audience, and has rapport and contacts with your target population. This individual helps link the researchers with locally influential people and others who can make later decisions about the study.

Seek Listeners

Consider the other skills that are needed from the volunteer team. You need volunteers who have the ability to listen carefully without interjecting their personal views. Not only must they listen, but they must also be able to relay those views without distortion to others on the research team. Some people are so eager and concerned about presenting their own views that they are unable or unwilling to listen to others. Seek those who can listen.

Pick Savvy People

Another valuable skill on the research team is people who "know how things work." These people have political savvy, understand complex human organizations, and know how and why human systems work the way they do. These people are valuable.

Sometimes, people hope that including naysayers on a research team will either encourage them to get with the collaborative program or at least keep their negative perspective visible. In our experience, such people can ruin the process at any point from beginning to end. It is better to create other ways to work with such individuals than to include them on the team itself.

Avoid Naysayers

Avoid the trap of taking only those who initially show interest in the study. Often the best people need to be persuaded to participate. Pick volunteers who have the capacity to listen to the bad news as well as the good, who are sociable, and who can leverage the results with decision makers.

Seek Talented Volunteers

Preparing the Team

Now the team must be prepared for the tasks ahead. We've found that a minimum of 4 hours is needed to prepare volunteers for uncomplicated studies.

As You Prepare the Team, You May Wish to Draw From Other Books in *The Focus Group Kit*. A Description of These Books Is on Pages xii-xiii.

• Train the team experientially. For a number of years, we had taught only adults to conduct focus group interviews. Then, we were invited to help a group of teens moderate some groups. One of the first changes we made was to increase the use of experiential exercises. We were so pleased with the results that we have increased the opportunities for all participants to practice and get feedback. Early on, our training sessions for adults consisted of about 30% to 40% practice experiences and 60% to 70% lecture. We reversed the ratio when working with teens, and we currently find that adult training with up to 50 percent experiential exercises yields positive results.

Our basic strategy in teaching consists of these steps:

1. An expert demonstrates
2. Discussion
3. Volunteers are invited to adapt and revise
4. A volunteer practices
5. Discussion and feedback
6. Repeat steps 4 and 5 as needed

This strategy and additional exercises are discussed in more detail in Chapter 3 of this volume.

In the training phase, it is important to share the study plan and invite amendments, particularly on logistics and questions. An important part of the training is an overview of the focus group questions. Volunteers need to feel comfortable asking the questions and need to understand the intent of each question. Moreover, volunteers need to become familiar with moderator skills, such as pausing, probing, or handling participants who are either too talkative or not talkative enough.

Identify the steps in the focus group interview, and consider having volunteers practice the various steps. In each case, the teacher might demonstrate, allow the student to adapt as needed, have the student demonstrate, and allow the teacher and other students to offer feedback. Here are areas that volunteers can practice:

A. Locating focus group participants
   1. Develop brainstorming strategies
   2. Find participants
   3. Identify selection problems
B. Recruiting focus group participants
   1. Identify appropriate incentives
   2. Prepare a draft invitation
   3. Conduct recruiting
C. Introducing the focus group
   1. Personalize the introduction
   2. Develop an ideal introduction
D. Developing questions
   1. Brainstorm potential questions
   2. Revise questions
E. Pilot testing questions
   1. Ask questions to volunteers
   2. Ask questions to friends
   3. Ask questions to members of the target audience
F. Moderating
   1. Observe a focus group
   2. Practice moderating
   3. Moderate a first group and get feedback
   4. Videotape a volunteer moderating a focus group
G. Note taking
   1. Demonstrate note taking
   2. Practice taking field notes
   3. Practice operating equipment
H. Transcribing
   1. Transcribe during the practice focus group
   2. Transcribe after the focus group

I. Giving the oral summary at the end of focus groups
   1. Practice the oral summary
   2. Have an expert and a volunteer work as a team
J. Analysis and report writing
   1. Have volunteers read analysis reports
   2. Have volunteers examine the analysis trail
   3. Observe the master
   4. Conduct the analysis of one group and receive feedback
   5. Conduct series analysis with feedback
K. Oral reporting
   1. Observe an expert giving an oral report
   2. Practice oral reports with the team
   3. Practice a one-to-one oral briefing

On the following pages, there are some examples of training schedules that we have found successful in working with volunteers. In the best of all possible worlds, everyone who conducts focus groups would be thoroughly trained with both knowledge and skills. Such thorough training is typically not possible for volunteers, given the multiple constraints on their time. Those who choose to use volunteers to conduct focus groups must accept this fact and create a training program that is as thorough and rigorous as time allows. Our experience suggests a minimal time allocation of 4 to 6 hours. Anything less than that truly may put the focus group process at risk. However, a range of possibilities exists for training experiences. We've included three training outlines which we call the brief, the moderate, and the extended schedules. The first outline is based on approximately 5 hours of training time. This schedule assumes that

- participants receive additional written background materials,
- the plan, questions, and logistics have been developed in advance, and
- participants will have limited or no opportunity to suggest modifications to the plan, questions, or logistics.

The major benefit of this brief schedule is that it seeks to offer volunteers a considerable amount of information in the shortest possible time period. The major limitation is that it doesn't allow time for revisions on core parts of the study. This plan works best when the problem is obvious, when the volunteer team members see the critical issues in similar ways, and when volunteer time is at a premium. The major risk of this plan is that it assumes that the volunteer team will accept, without reservation, the overall strategy. Often, volunteers, just like researchers, want to make changes in the study strategy, questions, or logistics. Because of this need to tinker with the study, researchers should anticipate how they might respond to suggestions for change. This risk can be minimized by involving volunteers in the planning and presentation of the training.

The second schedule makes fewer assumptions and allows more opportunity for the volunteers to offer suggestions and revisions. This second schedule requires about 10 hours and is presented over a period of several days. Often, we begin our planning with this second schedule as our model, and then, if time becomes limited, we move toward the briefer schedule. If more training time is possible, however, then we incorporate features of the third and most intensive training schedule.

The third schedule, which we call extended training, is most intensive and allows for considerable flexibility, but it requires approximately 50 hours—roughly that needed for a graduate research course in focus group interviewing. The third schedule has the time needed to develop questions, conduct the recruiting, and take on the time-consuming task of analysis. The third schedule assumes that volunteers will invest time in performing these tasks outside of the classroom.

Here are our suggested ingredients and practice exercises for each training schedule.

A. Brief Training Schedule—Five Hours (one day or two half-days)

Time (hours)	Topic
.5	Welcome, get acquainted, and build the team
.5	Explain the purpose of the study and describe the role of volunteers
1	Describe a generic focus group and demonstrate how it works Exercise F1—Observe a focus group

1	Outline specific expectations of volunteers
	    1. Work with a teammate
	    2. Recruit participants to the focus groups
	    3. Moderate focus groups using established questions
	        Exercise E1—Ask questions to volunteers
	        Checklist F5—Criteria for rating moderators
	    4. Capture information
	        Exercise G1—Demonstrate note taking
	        Exercise G3—Practice operating equipment

> Example G4—Standardized reporting form
> 5. Analyze and prepare summary report
>   Describe protocol and show examples
>   > Exercise J1—Have volunteers read analysis
>   > reports
> 6. Bring report to share with others
>   Describe reporting session
>   Set date and location of reporting session

1   Conduct a brief focus group on the topic with volunteers and debrief afterward

1   Summarize the logistics and make assignments

After the brief training, consider asking participants to continue improving their skills by doing some of the following exercises, described in Chapter 3.

> F2—Practice moderating
> F3—Moderate a first group with feedback
> F4—Videotape a volunteer moderating a focus group
> G2—Practice taking field notes
> H1—Transcribe during the practice focus group
> H2—Transcribe after the focus group
> I2—Have an expert and a volunteer work as a team
> J4—Conduct the analysis of one group and receive feedback

B. Moderate Training Schedule—Ten Hours (over several days)

Time (hours)	Topic
.5	Welcome, get acquainted, and build the team
1	Explain the purpose of the study and describe the role of volunteers
1.5	Describe a generic focus group and demonstrate how it works
	Exercise F1—Observe a focus group
4	An overview of what we want you to do
	1. Work with a teammate
	2. Recruit participants using an established protocol
	Exercise B1—Identify appropriate incentives
	Exercise B2—Prepare a draft invitation
	3. Moderate a focus group using established questions
	Describe and demonstrate introduction to focus group
	Exercise C1—Personalize the introduction
	Exercise C2—Develop an ideal introduction

Review critical skills of moderators
>   Checklist F5—Criteria for rating moderators
Present and explain proposed questions for focus group
>   Exercise E1—Ask questions to volunteers
>   Exercise F1—Observe a focus group
4. Take notes and record
Describe and demonstrate note taking
Present standardized reporting form (G4)
>   Exercise G1—Demonstrate note taking
>   Exercise G3—Practice operating
>   equipment
5. Analyze and prepare summary report
Describe process and show finished report
>   Exercise J1—Have volunteers read
>   analysis reports
6. Bring report to share with others
Describe reporting session
Set date and location of reporting session

2   Practice focus group on the topic
The researcher or master leads a focus group of five to seven
>   volunteers with remaining volunteers practicing other skills:
>   Exercise F1—Observe a focus group
>   Exercise G2—Practice taking field notes
>   Exercise I1—Practice the oral summary
1   Summarize logistics and make assignments

After the moderate training, consider asking participants to continue improving their skills by doing some of the following exercises. These exercises are described in Chapter 3.

B3—Conduct recruiting
D2—Revise questions
E2—Ask questions to friends
E3—Ask questions to members of the target audience
F2—Practice moderating
F3—Moderate a first group with feedback
F4—Videotape a volunteer moderating a focus group
H1—Transcribe during the practice focus group
H2—Transcribe after the focus group
I2—Have an expert and a volunteer work as a team
J3—Observe the master
J4—Conduct the analysis of one group and receive feedback

C. Extended Training Schedule—40 or More Hours
(multiple days spread over a term, quarter, or semester)

Class Time (hours)	Topic
2	Describing a generic focus group and how it works
2	Developing a study plan
2	Moderator skills
	Exercise F1—Observe a focus group
	Checklist F5—Criteria for rating moderators
2	Introducing the focus group
	Exercise C1—Personalize the introduction
4	Developing questions
	Principles and strategies for developing questions
	Exercise D1—Brainstorm potential questions
	Exercise D2—Revise questions
	Exercise E1—Ask questions to volunteers
	Exercise E2—Ask questions to friends
	Exercise E3—Ask questions to members of the target audience
2	Recruiting procedures—Selection, recruitment, and incentives
2-4	Practicing recruiting skills
	Exercise A1—Develop brainstorming strategies
	Exercise A2—Find participants
	Exercise B1—Identify appropriate incentives
	Exercise B2—Prepare a draft invitation
	Exercise B3—Conduct recruiting
2	Capturing information—Note taking and electronic recording
	Exercise G1—Demonstrate note taking
	Exercise G3—Practice operating equipment
1	Transcribing—Review transcribing strategies
2-4	Analyzing focus groups—Strategies for systematic analysis
	Exercise J1—Have volunteers read analysis reports
	Exercise J2—Have volunteers examine the analysis trail
2	Reporting focus group results—Styles and strategies
4-10	Getting ready for fieldwork—Practice focus groups
	F1—Observe a focus group
	F2—Practice moderating
	F3—Moderate a first group with feedback
	F4—Videotape a volunteer moderating a focus group
	G2—Practice taking field notes
	H1—Transcribe during the practice focus group

H2—Transcribe after the focus group

I1—Practice the oral summary

I2—Have an expert and a volunteer work as a team

J3—Observe the master

J4—Conduct the analysis of one group and receive feedback

J5—Conduct series analysis with feedback

K1—Observe an expert giving an oral report

K2—Practice oral reports with the team

K3—Practice a one-to-one oral briefing

10-20   Conducting the study

2-6   Reporting results

1-2   Summary of key points

An Overview of the Topics and Time Requirements for Three Training Options

Training Topics	Length of Training (in hours)		
	Brief	Moderate	Extended
Welcome, get acquainted, team development	.5	.5	
Explain purpose of study and general role of volunteers	.5	1	
Describe a generic focus group and demonstrate how it works	1	1.5	2
Specific expectations of volunteers	1 (recruit, moderate, capture information, analyze, report)	4 (recruit, moderate, capture information, analyze, report)	21-25 (plan, recruit, moderate, develop questions, capture information, analyze, report)
Practice focus group on the topic	1	2	4-10
Summarize logistics and make assignments	1	1	
Conduct the study, analyze, report results, conclude course			13-28
TIME ALLOCATED	5	10	40-65

Begin the Research

You're now ready to move into the field. The team is prepared, the final assignments are made, and the team is launched.

• Make assignments. Develop options for the team members and make assignments based on their skills and comfort. For example, we've often identified the following responsibilities:

> recruiter
>
> moderator
>
> assistant moderator
>
> analyst
>
> transcriber
>
> reporter

Let participants practice the skills before you make the final assignments. Specifically, let them practice the introduction to the focus group, taking notes in a focus group, and making a brief oral report of what was discussed.

Control the selection of moderators. Identify the skills needed, and then seek nominations from others. Some people should not moderate focus groups. They may have all the right demographic characteristics but lack certain basic communications skills that are essential for effective discussion. We remember one individual several years ago who was asked to help in a community focus group project. While everyone else dressed casually, he dressed in a suit and tie. Others were able to relax and exude a freedom to share, but this individual created an impression of rigidity. The individual did care about the community, but the image he presented did not foster what was needed in the more permissive focus group environment. In this case, we coached him into another role where his skills would be more beneficial to the study.

Have two people work together as a moderating team—a moderator and an assistant moderator. It may be that you pair a staff person with a volunteer; you can also pair volunteers. It helps to have two people for support, for backup, and for the different perspectives they bring. After the focus group, they can discuss what each heard. Having two people helps diminish bias that may creep in if only one person filters what is heard.

Without question, these decisions on the recruitment of volunteers and assignment of responsibilities involve subjective judgment. In making assignments, be diplomatic, gentle, and kind.

• Launch the team. A timetable is developed that is agreeable to the team. Now the team is ready to begin the study. Before they leave the training site, the team members should be familiar and comfortable with the expectations of them. Designate a coordinator to maintain contact and provide support for the team. This coordinator is the central contact for the duration of the study. This person maintains communication with team members, arranges substitutes when needed, and makes decisions on budgets, plans, and timing. He or she also alerts team members about new developments or modifications relating to the study.

The Training Plan

When conducting a study with a team of people, it is vital that the volunteers have a common understanding of the problem. Furthermore, the entire research team must be willing to tackle the problem as a team. If every person decides to pursue his or her personal interest, it is virtually impossible to make collective sense of the project. Therefore, we've found it necessary to prepare a training plan that conceptualizes the study and includes research instructions that are specifically tailored for a particular study.

This plan helps the research team move in step to ensure consistency and conformity. Occasionally, this training plan gets modified, and when this happens a new page is prepared and dated to insert into the training plan.

We offer a plan in the appendix as an example. Use it as a template, and modify it as needed. This is a plan that was actually put into action by a team of 25 volunteers, composed of university faculty, clerical staff, elected officials, and members of advisory committees.

Appendix
A Sample Training Plan

LISTENING TO CUSTOMERS
A guide for listening to customers and employees

TABLE OF CONTENTS

SPECIFIC TASKS

1. Purpose of the study

The purpose of this study is to inform and guide future decisions within the (name of organization) relating to:

- future directions of the (name of organization)
- observed and expected outcomes of the (name of organization)
- accountability and reporting of the (name of organization)
- unmet needs of customers
- level of satisfaction and dissatisfaction with the programs and operation of the (name of organization)

2. Specifications and key features of the study

- Creating a study team composed of volunteers and staff who will conduct approximately 20 focus groups throughout the state, each consisting of five to seven participants.
- A research-based approach to listening with systematic and verifiable procedures. This includes trained interviewers, consistent interviewing protocol, standardized questions, tape recording and field notes, reports for each focus group, and analysis by category and overall.
- A learning experience for 20 individuals. Increasingly, staff and volunteers need group processes and group listening skills. The skills developed in this study can be readily transferred to a variety of situations in communities, counties, or colleges.

3. Timeline

September	Training session
October	Recruiting
November	Conduct focus groups
December	Analyze and prepare reports; share results with team
January	Prepare final report

4. Target audiences

You will be assigned to conduct focus groups with one of the following target audiences. The target audiences are:

- Customers
  Individuals who have experienced programs from the (name of organization)

- Elected Officials
  County commissioners and state legislators

- Government Agency Staff
  Professionals from county, regional, state, and federal
    agencies

- Organization Staff
  Central office staff
  Field staff
  Support staff

5. **Expectations of the research team**

   5.1 Identify your teammate. Together, you and your team-
       mate will conduct two focus groups. You will each lead
       one and assist in one.

   5.2 Set the date, time, and location for the focus group
       interview.

   5.3 Inform the project coordinator (name of coordinator) of
       the date, time, and location. He or she will keep the
       master schedule and send the microphone before your
       focus group.

   5.4 Recruit (allow 2 weeks lead time)
       A. Invite people by phone or in person. Continue until
          seven or eight people have accepted. See invitation
          example in Section C of this appendix.
       B. Send a personalized letter to those accepting as soon
          as possible after they agree to participate. Note ex-
          ample in Section D of this appendix.
       C. Call to remind people the day before the session.

   5.5 Make name tents for participants

   5.6 Arrive early—at least 30 minutes before the session.
       Look over the room, make last-minute adjustments, set
       up equipment, test recording equipment, and put out the
       refreshments.

   5.7 Welcome people when they arrive. Place name tents
       around table. Ask participants to fill out the "Back-
       ground Information" page when they arrive. The
       "Background Information" page is in Section I of this
       appendix.

   5.8 Begin the focus group close to the time indicated. The
       assistant moderator greets latecomers and brings them
       into the group discussion.

   5.9 Debrief with assistant moderator. After participants have
       left, the moderator and assistant moderator should dis-
       cuss the findings. Check to see if the tape recorder

actually worked. Then, turn on the tape recorder and record your discussion. After the session, discuss:

- What were the high points, the most important concepts discussed?
- What quotes should be remembered?
- What was said that was not expected?
- How was this group different or similar from other groups?

Record these observations and any other thoughts you have that may be helpful in the analysis.

5.10 Return the microphone to (name of coordinator).

5.11 Analyze results. Within a few days after the focus group, prepare your analysis report. Send a copy to the assistant moderator for review and editing. Make changes as needed and send a copy, along with your field notes and the background information pages, to (name of coordinator).

5.12 Attend the reporting session. (Name of coordinator) will make copies of your report to share with other team members. Be prepared to give a short summary of your focus group.

6. Expectations of moderators

Before the focus group
- Coordinate recruitment.
- Coordinate logistics with your assistant moderator (room reservation, refreshments, tape recorder).
- Practice your introduction.
- Be comfortable with the questions.
- Be well rested.

During the focus group
- Arrive early.
- Determine seating around the table.
- Welcome people.
- Begin the group close to the designated time and conclude by the ending time.
- Monitor your time to be sure that all questions are discussed.
- Hold back your opinions.
- Avoid answering questions.

- Use pauses and probes to obtain information.
- Control your verbal and nonverbal reactions to participants.
- Use group facilitation skills.
- Ask the ending question: "Have we missed anything?"

After the focus group
- Conduct a debriefing.
- Listen to the tape, and prepare the written report.
- Send the report and analysis worksheet to (name of coordinator).
- Attend reporting session to:
  –share your oral report,
  –listen to reports of team members,
  –interpret results, and
  –develop recommendations.

7. **Expectations of assistant moderators**

Before the focus group
- Take responsibility for equipment. You will need a cassette tape recorder that has a jack for an external microphone. Also bring an extension cord for the tape recorder.
- Obtain refreshments and set them up in the room. Each focus group has a budget of $75, which includes room rental, refreshments, and child care.
- Rearrange chairs and table so everyone can see each other.

During the focus group
- Welcome participants as they arrive. Make small talk and introduce participants to each other.
- Sit in the designated location. The assistant moderator should sit outside the circle, opposite the moderator and close to the door. If someone arrives after the session begins, meet the person at the door, take him or her outside of the room, and give the individual a short briefing as to what has happened and the current topic of discussion. Then, bring the late participant into the room and indicate where to sit.
- Take notes throughout the discussion. Use the designated style for taking field notes.
- Monitor the recording equipment. Occasionally glance at the tape recorder to make sure the tape is moving. Label tapes so you will know their correct order later.

- Do not participate in the discussion. Talk only if invited by the moderator. Control your nonverbal actions no matter how strongly you feel about an issue.
- Ask questions when invited. At the end of the discussion, the moderator will invite you to ask questions of amplification or clarification.
- Give an oral summary. At the end of the discussion, the moderator or assistant should provide a brief summary (about 3 minutes) of responses to the important questions. Invite participants to offer additions or corrections. This oral summary is the first opportunity to highlight the key points of the discussion and obtain verification from participants.

After the focus group
- Participate in the debriefing with the moderator.
- Read and provide feedback on the report prepared by the moderator.
- Attend the reporting session.

SUGGESTIONS FOR SPECIFIC TASKS

A. Locating and recruiting strategies

Locate potential participants by using nominations, lists, or a piggyback process. Here are suggestions to help you.

Nominations

Individuals are nominated to participate in the focus group. Nominations can be obtained from advisory committee members or community leaders.

Suggestions when using nominations:
- Get more nominations than are needed because a number of people will have conflicts or not be interested in attending. Develop a pool of nominees, and then select randomly from that pool. To randomize, you might draw names from a hat or make a list and select every *n*th person (e.g., if you have 70 nominees and need to select 7 people, select every 10th person on the list).
- Usually, it is wise to mention the name of the person who made the nomination. For example: "John Doe recommended that we contact you and invite you to our discussion." Normally, the recruiter will tell nominees who nominated them. This seems to increase the legitimacy of the

study because it is being conducted by a reputable group and a friend or colleague made the nomination.

- Generally, it is best to seek nominations from several different people to minimize the potential for bias. If everyone is nominated by the same person, there is a greater tendency for the group members to share common opinions.
- Sometimes a participant may recommend another participant. Once again, be cautious about obtaining too many names from the same individual. Avoid people who live together or work closely together.

Lists

An individual's name appears on a membership or participation list. He or she may belong to some organization or have signed in when attending a meeting or activity.

Suggestions when using lists:
- Get the most up-to-date lists possible.
- Whenever possible, get a list with more information than just names, such as addresses, phone numbers, and any relevant demographic information or participation level.
- Randomly select names from the list.

Piggyback Selection

Focus groups can be conducted just before, during, or after another event, meeting, or activity. People attending the activity are asked to take several hours and participate in the focus group interview.

Suggestions when using piggyback selection:
- You may need approval from some individual, committee, or board to conduct focus groups during the conference or event.
- Attempt to get the best time possible for conducting the group. If you piggyback at a conference, you will usually not get a prime time. Most often, it will be in the late afternoon or evening when people are tired and desire some free time. Consider incentives.

When recruiting, be careful of . . .

Whatever the means you use to identify participants, be cautious about the following factors.

- Avoid inviting supervisors and subordinates in the same group. If people work in the same organization, then they should feel that they are at the same level as others in the focus group. The perceived power differential often limits free-flowing ideas.
- Avoid inviting spouses to the same focus group. Usually, only one will talk.
- Avoid inviting your close friends or relatives. You will be uncomfortable not sharing your opinion, and so will your friends or relatives.

B. Incentives

As you begin recruiting participants for the focus group, think about the experience from their point of view. Why should they attend? Why should they take it seriously? Don't assume that participants will be eager to attend. They may be fed up with meetings or cynical about the process. These factors may be helpful to consider when extending the invitation:

- A positive, upbeat invitation
  "We'd really like to have you join us."

- The opportunity to share opinions
  "You will be listened to. We want to hear from you."

- Good location
  "The location is enjoyable, convenient, and easy to find. It will be fun and comfortable. You will like it."

- Involvement in an important research project
  "Your opinions will count. Your ideas will help us."

- Community appeal. Build on existing community, social, or personal relationships.
  "Your participation will help benefit others."

- Food
  "We want you to be comfortable."

C. Sample telephone invitation (modify as needed)

Here's an example of words to use when inviting someone over the telephone to attend the focus group. Modify this to use words that are comfortable to you. Make it friendly and conversational.

"Hello, my name is _____ , and I am assisting the (name of organization) in a special study. We'd like to invite you to participate in a group discussion. The topic will be the (name of organization). Over the past few years, the (name of organization) has made changes in its programs. We want and need your opinions on these changes in order to help guide and inform future directions. We are inviting a small group of people from the community to join us for a discussion. The (name of organization) is concerned about listening to its customers, and you are one of those valued customers. The information you give us will be shared with the decision-making groups of the organization. The discussion will be on (date) at (time) and will be held at (location). Will you be able to join us?"

D. Sample letter of invitation (modify as needed)

Here's an example of a letter of invitation that would follow the telephone (or in-person) invitation. This letter confirms an individual's acceptance of the invitation and gives written details of the focus group.

L E T T E R H E A D

Date
Name
Address
City, State, Zip

Dear _____ ,

Thank you for accepting our invitation to attend the discussion at (name of location) in (city, address, etc.) We will be talking about your experiences with (name of organization). This is a study conducted by the (name of organization) to gain insights from customers and employees of the (name of organization). Over the past few years, this organization has made several changes in its programs and approach to education. We want and need your opinions on these changes to help guide and inform future directions.

The discussion will last two hours and will consist of about seven people with similar backgrounds. Refreshments will be available. I will be leading the discussion, and if you have further questions, feel free to call me at (phone number).

Sincerely,

Moderator name and signature

E. Beginning the focus group discussion

The first few moments in a focus group discussion are critical. In a brief time, the moderator must create a thoughtful, permissive atmosphere; provide the ground rules; and set the tone of the discussion. Much of the success of group interviewing can be attributed to the development of this open environment. Here's an example:

"Good evening, and welcome to our session. Thank you for taking the time to join our discussion of the (name of organization). My name is _____ , and I am . . . (describe what you do or how you are connected with the organization). Assisting me is _____, who is . . . (describe the affiliation of the assistant). We are here to listen to customers of the (name of organization). Each of you has had some experience with this organization, and we would like you to share your thoughts and opinions. This is one of a number of sessions that we are holding all over the state. The purpose of our study is to learn more about the interests and needs of our customers. This information will be an influential factor in the future decisions made by the (name of organization). Also, some changes have been make in this organization over the past few years, and we would like your thoughts on those changes.

There are no right or wrong answers but rather differing points of view. Please feel free to share your point of view, even if it differs from what others have said.

Before we begin, let me remind you of some of our procedures. Please speak up. We're tape recording the session because we don't want to miss any of your comments. If several people are talking at the same time, the tape will get garbled, and we'll miss your comments. Although we will be on a first-name basis tonight, our later reports will not include any names attached to comments. You may be assured of complete confidentiality. Keep in mind that we're just as interested in negative comments as in positive ones, and at times, the negative comments are the most helpful.

Well, let's begin. We've placed name cards on the table in front of you to help us all remember each other's names. Let's find out some more about each other by going around the room. Tell us your name, where you live, and what first comes to mind when you hear the words (name of organization)."

F. Questions to ask in the focus group

1. What are you hearing people say about (name of organization) in your community?
2. What outcomes or results from (name of organization) have you observed or heard about?
3. Think back to an experience with (name of organization) that was outstanding. Describe it. (Encourage storytelling.)
4. What has been your greatest disappointment with (name of organization)?
5. Who doesn't participate in the program of (name of organization)? (Pause and wait for answers.) Why don't they participate?
6. Let's talk about needs of people in the community and efforts of (name of organization) to meet those needs. What needs are addressed most effectively by this organization? (Pause and wait for answers.) What needs are being overlooked that it should address?
7. What are people saying about (name of organization's) cooperative efforts with other organizations?
8. In recent years, there has been increasing concern about accountability for all public programs. Taxpayers are concerned about what they are getting from their investment. What should (name of organization) do about accountability?
9. How would you measure (name of organization's) success?
10. (Name of organization) wants people more involved in designing, planning, conducting, and evaluating programs. Programs are better when local residents are involved as active partners. What will encourage active participation?
11. Think about all that we have talked about today. What do you think is most important for (name of organization) to keep doing?
12. Have we missed anything?

G. Note taking

Here are suggestions to help you take field notes.

* Note taking is a primary responsibility of the assistant moderator. The moderator is not expected to take written notes during the discussion.

- On each page of field notes, draw a vertical line down the center of the page. Quotes should be recorded on the right side of the line, and key points should be recorded on the left side of it. Use a separate page for each question and write the question at the top of the page.
- Make a sketch of the seating arrangement on the back side of the field notes.
- When capturing notable quotes, listen for those that are particularly well said. Capture word for word as much of the statement as possible. Listen for sentences or phrases that are particularly enlightening or that eloquently express a specific point of view. Place the name or initial of the speaker after the quotations. Usually, it is impossible to capture the entire quote, but capture as much as you can with attention to the key phrases. Use an ellipsis [. . .] to indicate that part of the quote is missing.
- In the key points section of the field notes (left side), write short phrases or key words that express the main ideas that are discussed. Place an asterisk by those points on which there is agreement among several people.
- Place your opinions, thoughts, or ideas on the back side of the field notes. If a question occurs to you that you would like to ask at the end of the discussion, write it down in a circle or box so you will remember it.
- Note the nonverbal activity. Watch for the obvious, such as nods, physical excitement, eye contact between certain participants, or other clues that may indicate the level of agreement, support, or interest.

H. Analysis and reporting process

- Prepare a three- to six-page summary of the discussion soon after the focus group. Set aside about 4 hours to do this task.
- Listen to the tape, and use the field notes of the assistant moderator.
- Prepare the summary in the following format:

   Question 1
     –Key points
     –Notable quotes

   Question 2
     –Key points
     –Notable quotes, etc.

- It is OK to used bulleted points as long as they are descriptive and understandable.
- Share the first copy of the analysis report with the assistant moderator for feedback. The assistant should be comfortable with the report and feel that it accurately describes the discussion. Incorporate feedback from the assistant moderator as needed.
- Send a copy of the analysis report and the field notes to (name of coordinator). She will make multiple copies of the report to share at the reporting meeting.
- Attend the reporting meeting, and give the highlights of your discussion.

I. Background information about participants

Make copies of this page, and ask participants to fill it out before the focus group begins.

Background Information

Age

( )   20s
( )   30s
( )   40s
( )   50s
( )   60s
( )   70 or over

Race

( )   African American
( )   American Indian
( )   Asian / Pacific Islander
( )   Hispanic / Latino / Chicano
( )   White
( )   Other

Gender

( )   Female
( )   Male

3

Learning Exercises

This chapter provides exercises that researchers may wish to use with a team of volunteers. These exercises are intended to provide background and build skills for a particular task. We don't expect or intend that all of these be used with volunteers; rather, researchers should pick those experiences most relevant to their team of volunteers. The experiences that we'll cover include 11 skill areas:

A. Locating focus group participants
B. Recruiting focus group participants
C. Introducing the focus group
D. Developing questions
E. Pilot testing questions
F. Moderating
G. Note taking
H. Transcribing
I. Giving an oral summary at the end of focus groups
J. Analysis and report writing
K. Oral reporting

For each of these skill areas, we will present background information helpful to instructors and then suggest exercises that prepare volunteers.

A. Locating Focus Group Participants

Volunteers often have advantages in locating participants because they have more local contacts than do researchers. For example, school principals know how to find other principals, and kids know how to locate other kids. Volunteers have credibility because they are from the community, they speak the language, they know the culture, and they are trusted. In some studies, this can make an enormous difference in recruiting.

Our intent is to find focus group participants who have the background and demographic characteristics specified in the study. Participants must meet established qualifications that focus group researchers call "screens." The difficulty of identifying participants is often underestimated, particularly in studies where lists of participants are unavailable or where people who meet the qualifications are unknown to the researchers.

A guiding principle is that the recruiter uses a systematic strategy to avoid bias in the selection process. It's important that prospective participants meet the established screening qualifications and that randomization be used to narrow the field of possibilities. If these principles are not followed, then researchers may be in doubt about the application of their findings.

The strategy for selection is straightforward. The recruiters need to develop a pool of people who meet the qualifications and then randomly select people from that pool. The size of the pool will vary depending on the difficulty of locating names. It is helpful to have four or five times more people in the pool than you need for your focus groups. In fact, in situations where you get a high refusal rate or scheduling conflicts, you may need 10 or even 20 times the number of focus group participants in the pool. For example, if you plan three focus groups and recruit eight people for each group, you'll need 24 participants agreeing to attend; in fact, you may need four or five times this number of names in your pool ($24 \times 4 = 96$) because a number of people will have conflicts or be unwilling to attend. The first task is to identify a pool of people who meet the screens and to do so as efficiently as possible.

We offer several exercises for your consideration. EXERCISE A1—DEVELOP BRAINSTORMING STRATEGIES is intended to tap into the insights of volunteers to identify potential focus group participants. EXERCISE A2—FIND PARTICIPANTS is intended to identify the action steps that volunteers might actually take to locate focus group participants. This exercise takes the discussion from an abstract idea to precise, concrete steps. EXERCISE A3—IDENTIFY SELECTION PROBLEMS is like a brainteaser. The problems and possible answers are intended to help volunteers to see how researchers "think" about these problems. Don't be surprised if volunteers offer other creative solutions or argue that the suggested answers just won't work in their environment. Have fun with this exercise. Use it as a springboard to additional examples. BACKGROUND A4— WHAT IS BIAS IN RECRUITING? gives background information on recruiting bias, and EXAMPLE A5—BIAS IN RECRUITING illustrates how bias was avoided in one focus group study. TIP A6—FINDING FOCUS GROUP PARTICIPANTS identifies three strategies that volunteers can use for locating participants. Finally, TIP A7—RANDOM SELECTION IN A CROWD offers tips on how to select people randomly from a crowd to participate in focus groups.

Brainstorm strategies for locating people. Invite volunteers to join you in a brainstorming session on locating people to participate in the study. You're not seeking to identify specific individuals, but general strategies for locating categories of people. Begin by reviewing the screening criteria and making a list of possible ways to locate participants. Following this procedure, choose one of these alternatives. Ask participants to pick those strategies that reliably and without bias identify the target audience and can be used in a practical manner, or agree as a group to use one of the strategies.

EXERCISE
_____

A1—Develop Brainstorming Strategies

Ask volunteers what they can do and would be willing to do to locate participants for the focus groups. This exercise can follow the previous exercise in which strategies were identified. This exercise is intended to discover practical and feasible strategies. The ideal strategy is worthless if no one will actually do it. The strategies most frequently used by volunteers are lists of participants, nominations, and piggybacking on other events or activities. The team leader might specifically ask the volunteers, "What are you able to do to locate participants? Would you locate a list? Would you seek nominations? Would you contact people in charge of an event and ask if focus groups can be conducted?"

EXERCISE
_____

A2—Find Participants

Here are questions to help volunteers think about minimizing bias and maintaining efficiency in the selection of participants. Ask these questions, letting volunteers discuss possible options. Some answers are mentioned here, but other answers are certainly possible.

Problem 1
_____

Here is a list of 200 names, in alphabetic order, of people who meet our screening requirements. How would you randomly select 50 people?

Possible answers:

- *Take every fourth person on the list.*

EXERCISE
_____

A3—Identify Selection Problems

- *Cut up the list so each name is on a separate piece of paper; put all of the names in a hat, mix up the pieces, and draw out 50 names.*
- *Number all names, and pick 50 numbers from a list of random numbers.*

Problem 2

Here is a list of 300 names in no known order. You don't know which ones meet the screening requirements. What would you do to achieve a random selection?

Possible answers:

- *Randomly select names, make phone calls, and use a screening questionnaire.*
- *Obtain demographic information from lists and from visits with knowledgeable local people. Then, randomly select names of those who have passed through the screens.*

Problem 3

You have 50 nominations and need to recruit 20 participants. How would you begin? Possible answers:

- *It depends on how the nominations were obtained. If they were obtained in a reasonably nonbiased manner, then just randomly select names from the list. If the list is biased, you may need to set it aside and seek out additional names.*
- *Be careful about selecting too many nominees from any one source. Get only a few nominees from each person offering nominations. If you have more, then randomly select a few names from each source.*

Problem 4

You are planning on conducting three focus groups of teachers in a school, and there are only 30 teachers in total to select from. How would you make your selection?

Possible answer:

- *Invite them all. Likely a few will be unable to attend, and if, by chance, too many want to attend, ask for feedback in person, in writing, or hold another focus group.*

BACKGROUND

A4—What Is Bias in Recruiting?

Recruiting bias occurs when certain individuals are included or excluded from the focus group for reasons not specified in the research plan. This bias raises the possibility that the results may be skewed because these individuals may hold points of view or opinions that are substantially different from a cross section of people who meet the screening requirements.

EXAMPLE

A5—Bias in Recruiting

The postal service conducted focus groups with employees around the country. These discussions were held during work hours, and supervisors needed to identify employees and then approve their release from work responsibilities to attend the focus groups. When supervisors were asked to help with recruiting, it was critical that clear and specific criteria be established to make selection easy for the supervisor and to avoid biasing the study. Without the criteria, some supervisors indicated that they would pick employ-

ees who were regular complainers just to let headquarters know what they as supervisors faced daily. Other supervisors indicated that they would recruit those who would not slow down the flow of the mail—what some felt were the less essential employees. Still other supervisors said they would select those who would offer headquarters sound and helpful advice, which often meant that their opinions were fairly similar to those of the supervisors. In each case, the supervisor would recruit participants who met the basic screens of position classification, employment history, and other demographics, but their attitudes, morale, and opinions might be extreme and unrepresentative.

Here are three strategies for finding focus group participants. When working with volunteers, we have found these three to be both practical and effective.

- Lists. Perhaps the most efficient way of finding names is to use an existing list. This could be a membership list or a list of attendees, employees, or students at school. Check to be certain that the list is current. Try to locate lists that include phone numbers, addresses, and other demographic data. This saves time in tracking down phone numbers and also allows you to select people by additional factors such as age, gender, and geographic location.

- Nominations. Nominations occur when community residents or others nominate people who might attend. A typical strategy is to go to locally influential people, tell them your purpose, and ask them to suggest the names of people who meet the qualifications. Ask them for nominations, but not for people to attend. Do not promise that every person suggested will be invited. Say instead that these names will go into a pool and then participants will then be randomly selected from that pool. To minimize bias, it is important to seek nominations from a variety of different informants. Keep track of who was suggested by whom because you may want to mention this person when you contact the nominee.

- Piggyback or on-location recruiting. The piggyback strategy is used when participants are gathered together for a different, unrelated purpose and you ask them to join you in a focus group. They may be attending a professional meeting, a conference, or a workshop, and just before, during, or after the event, they are asked to participate in the group. On-location focus groups occur at events, festivals, fairs, or similar activities that bring together many people from a community. Recruiting for piggyback or on-location focus groups can use the procedures discussed above for the list or nominations, particularly if the recruiting is held in advance of the event or activity. However, if recruiting is held during the event, the recruiting team will need to devise a random-type protocol for selection. ICON A7 offers suggestions on making random selections within a crowd. Caution is sometimes needed. Getting volunteers in an open meeting can be biased because those who step forward may hold extreme positions or be different in important ways that can affect the study.

TIP

A6—Finding Focus Group Participants

Here are some ways to select focus group participants randomly from a large group of people.

- Invite every nth person who walks through the door.
- Randomly select names in advance and "tag" these names for recruitment at registration. When they arrive to register, invite them to participate.

TIP

A7—Random Selection in a Crowd

- *Place marks under certain chairs; ask those who sit in these designated places to participate in focus groups.*
- *Select an entire subgroup of people who meet the screening criteria, but be careful of other biases that may emerge. This might be a subcommittee, a special-interest section, or some other biased grouping.*
- *Ask subgroups to identify volunteers who meet the requirements.*

B. Recruiting Focus Group Participants

Recruiting can be a terrible job. It can be frustrating, time-consuming, and inefficient. The goal in using volunteers is to capitalize on their assets and make the task as pleasant as possible. The attitude that you should convey in recruiting is one of respect and honor, not the idea of randomness in selection or that someone is just another person in the crowd. Those invited possess wisdom and insight that will benefit others, the community, or the study. The focus group gives participants an opportunity to share their insights. This respectful attitude needs to be reflected in the words the recruiter uses. Volunteers usually have valuable contacts and are trusted within their communities, whether a geographic community, a social community, or a professional community. What's needed is a strategy that is both effective (the right people say "yes" to the invitation) and efficient (a sizable number say "yes" quickly). Part of what makes an invitation successful is that it comes from the right person, is upbeat and positive, offers sufficient information about the focus group, and is individualized to the participant.

Recruiting can occur in several ways. It can be through one-to-one contacts at a festival, gathering, community event, work, or school, but often it is on the telephone. People are more likely to participate in a group if they feel the study relates to their interests and concerns. The recruiter needs to let potential participants know why they were invited and how their name was selected. The first contact with potential participants is often on the telephone or in person. Sometimes, a written invitation is sent out, informing potential participants that they may soon receive an invitation to offer their opinions for a study or on an issue of importance.

We suggest three exercises. EXERCISE B1—IDENTIFY AP-PROPRIATE INCENTIVES can be used in a brainstorming manner to discover new and creative ideas or to weigh the pros and cons of alternative incentives. In EXERCISE B2—PREPARE A

DRAFT INVITATION, volunteers offer their suggestions for what to include in the invitation to participate. EXERCISE B3—CONDUCT RECRUITING is the actual process of finding people to participate. This exercise is made easier by the use of TIP B4—INVITE PEOPLE TO OFFER THEIR OPINIONS. Sometimes, it is necessary to use a screen to locate participants, prior to offering the invitation. EXAMPLE B5—SAMPLE TELEPHONE SCREENING SCRIPTS provides examples of screens. When using the telephone for recruiting, you might consider developing rules or guidelines to ensure consistency and avoid problems. TIP B6—SUGGESTED RECRUITING GUIDELINES offers several possible rules. Finally, EXAMPLE B7—TELEPHONE LOG FOR RECRUITING is helpful because it eliminates embarrassing duplicate calls and provides a format for volunteers to track their contacts.

Ask volunteers to identify recruitment incentives. What's needed to make sure participants actually attend? Volunteers might consider the appropriateness and need for incentives such as money, food, gifts, and feelings of involvement and serving a community need.

EXERCISE

B1—Identify Appropriate Incentives

Ask volunteers to help prepare a draft invitation. This invitation should convey a conversational, upbeat, and friendly approach. One way to prepare this script is to tape volunteers as they practice their invitations. The tapes are then transcribed, and the best sections are included in the draft script. The outline of the invitation might include wordings like the following:

EXERCISE

B2—Prepare a Draft Invitation

- *We need your help. We want your opinions, ideas, views.*
- *We want you to join us in a discussion of an important topic.*
- *The topic is . . .*
- *The topic is important because . . .*
- *We want your help because you are . . .*
- *It will be at (location) during (time).*
- *The discussion is sponsored by . . .*
- *The results will be used for . . .*
- *We will be offering (incentive) . . .*
- *Will you be able to join us?*

Then, ask the entire team of volunteer recruiters to review the composite script and adapt it as needed. Once again, ask volunteers to practice the script on each other, and allow them to modify the script to use words and phrases that are most comfortable to them. Tape record and play back these recruiting conversations. Your goal is to achieve consistency while remaining upbeat and conversational, so that all of the people invited to the focus group have similar and consistent background on the purpose, sponsorship, and uses of the study. Allow the research team to decide which modifications are acceptable. Don't insist that everyone use exactly the same script. Instead, allow for variations as long as they are deemed by the recruiting team to be sufficiently similar. Note EXERCISE B5 with examples of recruiting scripts.

EXERCISE

B3—Conduct Recruiting

In this exercise, volunteers actually conduct the recruiting. The volunteer recruiters should stay in touch with the researcher to monitor their progress and receive any special instructions that may emerge as the recruiting progresses. The researcher should develop written protocols to guide the volunteer recruiters. Note the suggestions in TIP B6 on recruiting guidelines and in EXERCISE B7—TELEPHONE LOG FOR RECRUITING.

TIP

B4—Invite People to Offer Their Opinions

Occasionally, the first contact with participants is made in writing. Typically, it is a letter informing them that a study is under way and that they may be asked to participate. It's difficult to know how many should receive the invitation and the extent to which you should overrecruit. Here's one solution. When using written invitations, don't invite the people to a focus group but rather to offer their thoughts and opinions. Some people will be requested to participate in a discussion, and others will be requested to give their views in writing. After you have invited the necessary number to the focus group in the phone calls that follow the initial letters, the remainder of the people receive the open-ended, mail-out survey containing the focus group questions in survey form. With this procedure, you don't need to worry about over recruiting. Recruit as many people as you need, and ask the remainder to respond to the study questions in writing. The results are analyzed separately. This way, each person feels connected with the study and is not upset if he or she is not invited to the focus group.

EXERCISE

B5—Sample Telephone Screening Scripts

Telephone screening questionnaire
Example 1
Parents of teenagers

Interviewee Name _____   *Date* _____

*Address*_____   *Phone (   )_____*

Hello, my name is _____*, and I'm calling from the University of Minnesota in St. Paul. We are conducting a short survey of parents of teenagers. Are you a parent of a teenager?*

[IF YES, CONTINUE. IF NO, ASK FOR A PARENT.]

We are conducting a family survey that will take less than two minutes. Is it OK to begin?

    1. How many children who are between ages 13 and 18 currently live with you?
      _____ *Number*

      (   ) None. Thank you, we have no further questions.

2. What type of school do the teenagers in your home attend?
   Is it public, private, or home school?

   _____ Public school [Recruit six]

   _____ Private school [Recruit six]

   _____ Home school [Recruit six]

We are asking selected people to join us for a discussion about raising teenagers. We're interested in how parents work together with schools and other groups and organizations within the community. We'd like to have your views. The information will be used to develop tips and suggestions to help parents. The discussion will be at the _____ on _____ at _____ and will last two hours. Coffee and rolls will be served. Would you be able to join us at that time?

   ( ) Yes   Name: _____

   ( ) No   Thank you for answering our questions.

[IF YES] I will be sending you a letter confirming this information. Should I use the address of _____? [CONFIRM ADDRESS] If you need any help with directions or if you need to cancel, please call our office at 234-5678. Thank you very much for your cooperation.

Telephone screening questionnaire
Example 2
Working women between 25 and 49 in Fairview County

Interviewee Name _____ Date _____

Address_____ Phone ( )_____

Hello, my name is _____, and I'm calling for Northern Research in Minneapolis. We are conducting a short survey in Fairview County of women who work outside of the home. Is such a person available?

[IF AVAILABLE, CONTINUE. IF NOT, TERMINATE.]

Northern Research is conducting a study on informal education in Fairview County, and I would like to ask you a few questions. The questions will take less than two minutes. Is it OK to begin? First, let me ask your name? _____

1. Do you live in Fairview County?

   ( ) Yes [CONTINUE]

   ( ) No [TERMINATE]

2. Are you employed full-time or part-time?

   ( ) Full-time [CONTINUE]

   ( ) Part-time [TERMINATE]

3. In what age category do you belong?

    ( ) Under 25 [TERMINATE]

    ( ) 25–34 [RECRUIT AT LEAST 8]

    ( ) 35–49 [RECRUIT AT LEAST 8]

    ( ) 50 or over [TERMINATE]

[PARTICIPANT RECRUITMENT]

Ms. _____, Northern Research is sponsoring a meeting with working women in Fairview County to discuss informal education. We know that working women are busy, and yet they get new information and education from a variety of sources. We would like you to join a group of other working women to discuss this topic. This is not a sales meeting but strictly a research project. It will be held on Thursday evening, December 3rd, at the Riverside Restaurant in Conover. We would like you to be our guest for dinner, which will begin at 7:00 p.m. The meeting will be over at 9:30 p.m. Will you be able to attend?

    ( ) Yes   [CONFIRM NAME AND ADDRESS]

    ( ) No   [THANK AND TERMINATE]

[IF YES] I will send you a letter in a few days confirming this meeting. If you need any help with directions or if you need to cancel, please call our office at _____. Thank you, and good-bye.

B6—Suggested Recruiting Guidelines

Prepare recruiting guidelines to ensure consistency and efficiency. Among those you might consider are:

- Keep a phone log of the people you've called, when you called, and the status of the call. At a glance, you can determine how many are completed and how many remain.

- Make three attempts to reach an individual. In some situations, where it is vital to have a specific individual, you might make more attempts.

- Don't encourage return calls unless absolutely essential. If the potential participant isn't available, ask when would be a good time to call back and then call again at that time. If you encounter an answering machine, leave a message that you've called and when you plan to call back. In a few situations, you might indicate a time and phone number when you can be called back. Don't do this very often, because it is impractical and inefficient to hold space at a focus group while you are waiting for people to return your phone calls.

- Use local traditions when deciding when to make phone invitations. In some communities, the phones are used after 9:30 or 10:00 p.m. only in emergencies or by teens. Mealtimes can vary greatly from one community to another, and, if known, these times might be avoided. Generally, professional callers disregard meal hours because of the diversity of eating times and to achieve maximum efficiency in calling.

TELEPHONE LOG				
Caller's Name:				
Name & Address	Phone Number	Date/Time Called	Status	Notes
Bob Smith 1234 Elm Anytown, State 12345	444-5678	9-27 4 p.m.	Accepted	
Delores Jones 45 State St. Priorville, State 12346	555-6789	9-27 4:10 p.m. 9-27 6:30 p.m. 9-27 8:10 p.m.	No answer No answer No answer	
Mary Johnson 123 47th Ave. Anytown, State 12345	444-9876	9-27 4:20 p.m.	Declined	
Pat Conners 456 23rd St. Anytown, State 12345	444-2378	9-27 4:30 p.m.	Left message on answering machine	Call back about 8:00 p.m. on 9-27.
Kim O'Brien Box 34 Oakville, State 12347	443-7654	9-27 4:35 p.m.	Left message	Call back about 7:30 p.m. on 9-27.
Roland Thomas 235 State St. Priorville, State 12346	443-3210	9-27 4:45 p.m.	Accepted	Change mailing address to 235 Stage St.

EXAMPLE

**B7—Telephone
Log for Recruiting**

C. Introducing the Focus Group

The first few moments of the focus group are critical. In a brief time, the moderator must create a thoughtful, permissive atmosphere; describe the ground rules; and set the tone of the discussion. Much of the success of group interviewing depends on these first few minutes.

The strategy is to present a friendly and relaxed introduction to the focus group. This introduction sets the tone of the group and provides the operating guidelines for the discussion. Each volunteer will have different talents and ways of extending the introduction. Not every moderator needs to use exactly the same words, but the content of what's said should be consistent across all focus groups in a series.

The typical introduction includes four points: a welcome, an overview of the topic, the guidelines for the discussion, and the opening question.

We've included two exercises to help volunteers with their introduction to the focus group. The first, EXERCISE C1—PERSONALIZE THE INTRODUCTION, is intended to help volunteers become comfortable with the flow of the introduction and to allow them to use their own words when introducing the study. It can be awkward to present an introduction developed by someone else. Participants around the table quickly sense that something is amiss. By allowing volunteers to present the introduction in their own way, you are able to capture creative and effective approaches. Be careful, however, because if everyone has a different approach, there is the danger that you will lose comparability among focus groups. A degree of consistency from one group to another is needed to ensure that each participant has equivalent background information and instruction on the study. To achieve this, we offer EXERCISE C2—DEVELOP AN IDEAL INTRODUCTION. In EXERCISE C2, the group of volunteers works together to identify the phrases, sections, or words that go into a composite introduction. This "ideal introduction" is then prepared in writing and shared with the team as a model. EXAMPLE C3—SCRIPT OF A FOCUS GROUP INTRODUCTION and EXAMPLE C4—BULLETED OUTLINE OF A FOCUS GROUP INTRODUCTION may be helpful to volunteers as they prepare their introductions. CHECKLIST C5—CHECKLIST FOR FOCUS GROUP INTRODUCTIONS can be used by volunteers to critique each other, particularly in EXERCISE C1.

EXERCISE

C1—Personalize the Introduction

Invite volunteers to develop their own scripts. Let them look over a standard script, such as the one included in EXAMPLE C3. Encourage them to personalize the script with words that are comfortable to them and appropriate to the audience. Some may wish to write out their introductions, and others may wish to use the bulleted points in EXAMPLE C4. Give each volunteer an opportunity to practice his or her introduction with other volunteers. Often, we'll sit around a table and ask each volunteer to offer his or her introduction and receive feedback. After each introduction, offer comments on the words used and the style of delivery. Consider using the checklist for focus group introductions included in CHECKLIST C5. Also consider using a video camera to capture the introduction, and then play back the video for the volunteer.

EXERCISE

C2—Develop an Ideal Introduction

Develop a common script that is a composite of the best sections from each volunteer's version. After all of the volunteers give their presentations, ask the volunteer team which introductions should be transcribed and used as models for others. In the past, we have taken a paragraph from one volunteer, a phrase from another, and a word or two from still another. We put these together in a suggested written introduction that can be reviewed and practiced by the volunteers.

"Good evening, and welcome to our session tonight. Thank you for taking the time to join our discussion of airplane travel. My name is [insert name], and I represent the Happy Traveler Research Agency. Assisting me is [insert name], also from the Happy Traveler Agency. We want to hear how public employees feel about airplane travel. We're invited people who work in different governmental agencies to share their thoughts and ideas.

You were selected because you have certain things in common that are of particular interest to us. You are all government employees who work here in the metropolitan area, and you have all traveled by air at least four times in the past year. We are particularly interested in your views because you have had lots of experience traveling, and we want to hear about those experiences.

Today, we'll be discussing your experiences and opinions about airline travel. There are no wrong answers but rather differing points of view. Please feel free to share your point of view, even if it differs from what others have said.

Before we begin, let me suggest some things that will make our discussion more productive. Please speak up—only one person should talk at a time. We're tape recording the session because we don't want to miss any of your comments. If several people are talking at the same time, the tape will get garbled, and we'll miss your comments. We'll be on a first-name basis, but in our later reports there will not be any names attached to comments. You may be assured of confidentiality. Keep in mind that we're just as interested in negative comments as positive comments, and at times the negative comments are the most helpful.

My role here is to ask questions and then to listen. I won't be participating in the conversation, but I want you to feel free to talk with one another. We've placed name cards on the table in front of you to help us remember each other's names. Let's begin. Let's find out some more about each other by going around the table. Tell us your name, your favorite place you've traveled to in the past year, and what made it your favorite."

EXAMPLE

C3—Script of a Focus Group Introduction

- Welcome
  - Introduce moderator and assistant
- Our topic is . . .
  - The results will be used for . . .
  - You were selected because . . .
- Guidelines
  - There are no wrong answers, only differing points of view.
  - We're tape recording, one person speaking at a time.
  - We're on a first-name basis.
  - You don't need to agree with others, but you must listen respectfully as others share their views.
  - Rules for cellular phones and pagers, if applicable. For example: We ask that your turn off your phones or pagers. If you cannot, and if you must respond to a call, please do so as quietly as possible and rejoin us as quickly as you can.
  - My role as moderator will be to guide the discussion.
  - Talk to each other.
- Opening question

EXAMPLE

C4—Bulleted Outline of a Focus Group Introduction

NAME _____

CHECKLIST

C5—Checklist for
Focus Group
Introductions

CHECKLIST FOR FOCUS GROUP INTRODUCTIONS			
	RATING		
CONTENT	*Change this*	*No change needed*	*COMMENTS*
Extends a welcome			
Introduces moderator and assistant			
Introduces study—why we're here			
Describes how participants were selected			
Welcomes all points of view			
Provides ground rules			
We're recording—confidentiality assured			
No invitation for questions			
Appropriate opening question			
Appropriate word choice			

DELIVERY	*Change this*	*No change needed*	*COMMENTS*
Relaxed and friendly			
Conveys sincerity and trust			
Smiles at some point			
Speed appropriate for participants			
Eye contact			
No distractions from content			

Suggestions for improvement

D. Developing Questions

Volunteers help ensure that the questions are appropriate for the audience and that the questions truly ask what is intended. Good questions are the heart of the focus group. Questions must be clear, brief, reasonable, and asked in a conversational manner. Furthermore, questions must be asked in a consistent way across the team of moderators. Therefore, it's of value for volunteers to provide advice in the development of questions, to critique drafts of the proposed questions, and to be fully comfortable with the final version of questions. Questions that are not familiar or comfortable to the moderator are doomed to failure.

Quality questions are developed with the help of a team, which is usually composed of researchers, volunteers, and selected members of the target audience.

We suggest two exercises that have been helpful in developing and finalizing the questions for a focus group. These exercises are D1—BRAINSTORM POTENTIAL QUESTIONS and D2—REVISE QUESTIONS. By using these two exercises together, you will be able to obtain a rich breadth of input from a number of people but not be saddled with having the group make specific decisions on each question. Groups are good for suggesting ideas and for responding to sets of questions. Groups are not good for crafting specific questions. TIP D3—KEEP TRACK OF YOUR REVISIONS suggests a strategy for avoiding confusion due to multiple revisions.

For More Information on Developing Questions, Read Chapter 3 in *Developing Questions for Focus Groups*

KEY POINT

Groups Are Good for Suggesting Ideas for Questions and Responding to Sets of Questions. Groups Are Not Good for Crafting Specific Questions.

Begin with a review of the problem, situation, or factors that are prompting the study. Once the problem is understood, the next step is to gather ideas for questions that will shed light on the problem. Brainstorming works well with a group of four to six people, and it is desirable to include volunteers. Later, the researcher should prepare the first draft of the questions.

EXERCISE

D1—Brainstorm Potential Questions

Share drafts of questions with volunteers, and revise, revise, revise. Volunteers should be asked to review and offer feedback on improving the questions. Feedback is inevitable, and it improves the questions. The challenge is to bring closure to the feedback at the right time and to move the study forward expeditiously. Remember to keep track of revisions as described in TIP D3.

EXERCISE

D2—Revise Questions

When seeking feedback on questions, place the date at the bottom or top of each page to identify the revision. Don't be surprised if you have six to ten revisions before you bring closure on the questions. These date identifiers help the research team, clients, and others keep revisions separate.

TIP

D3—Keep Track of Your Revisions

E. Pilot Testing Questions

Sometimes words don't communicate what we intend. The purpose of pilot testing questions is to ensure that our questions have consistent and predictable meaning to focus group participants as well as to members of the research team. The answers to questions should come relatively quickly, be on target, and be useful to the study.

The strategy is to test the questions orally, just as they would be used in the focus group. Earlier, volunteers reviewed the questions in a written form. Now we find out if the questions work when asked aloud. First, let's consider the asking of the question. Does it sound awkward when asked orally? Do the words flow smoothly? Does it sound conversational? By tone and inflection, the moderator places emphasis on certain key words in the question. Is this emphasis correct? Second, this exercise helps give insight into potential responses. The responses should shed light on the topic of examination. If they don't, consider revision. Responses should occur relatively quickly and usually without undue delay. This exercise also helps in analysis because it identifies responses that might be anticipated.

We suggest three exercises to pilot test the questions. If at all possible, try to do all three. They are: EXERCISE E1—ASK QUESTIONS TO VOLUNTEERS, EXERCISE E2—ASK QUESTIONS TO FRIENDS, and EXERCISE E3 —ASK QUESTIONS TO MEMBERS OF THE TARGET AUDIENCE. Something is learned from each step, and each step is relatively simple. Begin by testing the questions on the volunteers. This step not only tests the actual questions, but it enables the volunteers to become familiar with the intent and helps them anticipate responses. The pilot test with friends and neighbors is easy to do and offers insights from people unfamiliar with the study. The most important pilot test, however, is with the target audience. Place the greatest weight on the results of the target audience pilot test. In each of the pilot tests, as well as in the focus groups, give careful thought to the answers. CAUTION EXERCISE E4—DID THEY ANSWER THE QUESTION? warns novice moderators of a common moderating difficulty. BACKGROUND E5—NOT EVERYONE THINKS THE SAME WAY offers another suggestion that will help novice moderators.

EXERCISE

E1—Ask Questions to Volunteers

Invite volunteers to ask the questions of each other, but do it so the research team can listen and observe. Give everyone a written copy of the questions, but with only the person asking the question looking at the script. Everyone else is listening because that is how the question will be used in the focus group. The exercise begins when someone is asked to read the first question. This person picks someone else from the group to answer the question. The question is asked, and then the respondent attempts to answer. When the answer is completed, we ask two questions: First, to the person asking the question, "How comfortable were you asking the question?" Then, to the person answering, "How comfortable were you with answering the question?" The listeners critique both the question and the delivery of the question. Was the correct emphasis placed on the right words? The question should flow smoothly and comfortably from the moderator. Furthermore, the oral version should place emphasis on the important words so that the intended message is communicated. The entire group might reflect on the degree to which the question was actually answered.

Ask friends, neighbors, or family members to answer the questions. Each member of the research team might try one or more questions with someone close and convenient. This exercise assumes that the topic is one of widespread interest and that these people might actually have some insight into the questions being asked. If the question relates to teens, then ask your teenage child or a neighbor teen to offer answers.

EXERCISE

E2—Ask Questions to Friends

Ask members of the target audience to answer the questions. Find an individual who meets the qualifications for participation in the focus group. This person is one who will not be selected to participate in the later study.

EXERCISE

E3—Ask Questions to Members of the Target Audience

A mistake often made by novice moderators is assuming that people are answering a question just because they are talking. There is a big difference between talking and answering the question. It is helpful to think of questions as a stimulus-response phenomenon. The question stimulates a participant to respond. However, it's hard to know what exactly the stimulus is. It may be a word, a phrase, the moderator's tone of voice, or something from the previous question. Ideally, the response is from an understanding of the entire question. Sometimes, listening is imperfect, and a participant might only catch a phrase and miss the broader intent of the question. Some participants talk even though they really don't know the answer. At times, the moderator is unable to determine the connection between the question and the response. When this occurs, the moderator needs to make a decision. Should I probe for clarification, or should I rephrase the question and ask it again? Doing nothing is risky because this comment can stimulate other comments, and soon the entire conversation may be off track and wasting valuable time.

CAUTION

E4—Did the Participant Answer the Question?

There are typically two types of people in focus groups. There are those who think first and then respond, and those who think and respond simultaneously. People in this second category need to talk in order to think. They don't know what they're going to say until they've said it. This has implications for moderators and analysts. Moderators and analysts need to remember that focus group participants will vary. Allow for and respect these differences. Some participants will be absolutely consistent, clear, and concise. Others will seem to ramble, reverse themselves, and go in different directions simultaneously. You may need to allow some participants to talk more in order to "find themselves" and then follow up with these people to determine their level of commitment or support for the ideas they've expressed. Just don't assume that everyone is or should be the same. Not everyone thinks the same way, and that's part of the joy of being human.

BACKGROUND

E5—Not Everyone Thinks the Same Way

F. Moderating

For More Information on Moderating, Look Over Volume 4 in This Series, *Moderating Focus Groups*

The moderator's role is to get people to talk about their opinions and experiences. The moderator creates a pleasant, nonthreatening environment, asks questions, probes and seeks examples as needed, and then gets all of the participants to share their views. This role is played out differently depending on the personality and background of the moderator.

The best way to prepare someone to moderate is first to demonstrate and then to let him or her practice. The demonstration is invaluable. It immediately helps the volunteer to grasp the strategy and the role of the moderator and the atmosphere of a group. If possible, allow volunteers to observe several master moderators to see variations on how they follow up, involve participants, respond to them, and generally apply the skills of moderating. (We will be using the words *master, mentor, coach,* and *expert* more or less interchangeably.)

The first exercise, EXERCISE F1—OBSERVE A FOCUS GROUP, may be the most single important exercise for beginning volunteers. This exercise vividly demonstrates the critical components of a focus group in a way that just cannot be done with words or writings. When the first exercise is finished, volunteers are often ready to practice. This is described in EXERCISE F2—PRACTICE MODERATING. If time and resources are available, the next two exercises are helpful: EXERCISE F3—MODERATE A FIRST GROUP WITH FEEDBACK and EXERCISE F4—VIDEOTAPE A VOLUNTEER MODERATING A FOCUS GROUP. CHECKLIST F5—CRITERIA FOR RATING MODERATORS is intended to remind volunteers of the array of tasks necessary to diagnose volunteer needs and identify volunteer skills.

EXERCISE

F1—Observe a Focus Group

Conduct a focus group with volunteers as the participants. The topic could be related to the research study or a neutral topic of interest to all. If possible, conduct several shorter focus groups (20 to 40 minutes long) using different master moderators. This experience may be the single most beneficial of all of the practice exercises because, in the brief example, the volunteers actually experience a focus group. Once everyone has observed the common focus group experience, you can add to the exercise by conducting additional practice groups with specific assignments. Ask some volunteers to be in the focus groups and others to serve as assistants, practice taking notes, and prepare short, ending summaries, which will be discussed later in this chapter. After each focus group, conduct a discussion of what the volunteers have seen and learned in the group.

Once the volunteers have observed an expert, let them try their hand at leading a focus group. Let volunteers practice moderating a group with other volunteers serving as participants. Once again, the topic can be related to the research study or any other topic of interest to the volunteers. This practice session should be critiqued by the coach or mentor, as well as by the other volunteers. Consider videotaping the volunteer moderator and playing back the session before discussing it.

EXERCISE

F2—Practice Moderating

The next level of volunteer skill development is to moderate a first focus group. Ideally, it is best to have the master or coach serve as an assistant moderator and offer feedback to the volunteer after the participants leave. If the master or coach is not available, then another volunteer can serve as assistant moderator and coach the beginning moderator. Consider using the moderator rating criteria in CHECKLIST F5.

EXERCISE

F3—Moderate a First Group With Feedback

Video tape a volunteer conducting a focus group. The volunteer places the video camera at eye level, tells the participants that he or she is interested in improving at moderating, and that the camera is pointed just at the moderator, not at them. At the end of the focus group, the volunteer asks the participants for their advice. Later, the volunteer watches the tape and does a self-critique using the moderator rating criteria in CHECKLIST F5. Invite a mentor or coach to help with the critique.

EXERCISE

F4—Videotape a Volunteer Moderating a Focus Group

Before the focus group

☐ Is familiar with the topic and goals of the sponsor

☐ Understands the purpose and objective of each question

☐ Has a sense of the amount of time needed for each question

☐ Anticipates the topics of discussion and potential areas of probing

☐ Is mentally and physically ready to moderate

☐ Has sufficient technical knowledge of the topic

☐ Welcomes participants and makes them feel comfortable before the session

CHECKLIST

F5—Criteria for Rating Moderators

During the focus group

☐ Delivers a smooth, comfortable introduction that is accurate and complete, including:

- a welcome

- a brief overview of the topic that defines the purpose of the group

- a description of the ground rules

- the opening question

☐ *Establishes rapport with participants*

☐ *Asks the questions as intended, unless they have already been answered in another question*

☐ *Allows sufficient time for each question*

☐ *Keeps the discussion on track*

☐ *Keeps all participants involved*

☐ *Listens carefully; synthesizes information and feeds it back, probes for clarification, gets people to talk.*

☐ *Seeks out both cognitive and affective domains; gets participants to tell both how they think and how they feel about the topic.*

☐ *Moves smoothly from one question to another*

☐ *Handles different participants adeptly and conveys a sense of relaxed informality.*

☐ *Avoids sharing personal opinions*

☐ *Finishes on time*

☐ *Brings closure to the group with a summary and invites comments on any missing points*

☐ *Goes to the door and thanks each person individually for coming, just as you would when guests leave your home*

After the focus group

☐ *Debriefs soon after the focus group with the assistant moderator*

☐ *Performs the analysis or provides insight into the analysis*

☐ *Reviews the report for accuracy*

G. Note Taking

Everyone has had experience with taking notes, but rarely are we given guidance about what notes to take and how to do so effectively and efficiently. The objective of note taking is to document what actually occurred in the focus group. Memories are faulty and limited, no matter how capable the researcher. Therefore, information is usually captured both by written field notes and by tape recordings. Other alternatives also exist, such as flip charts, real-time transcripts made on a laptop computer, or video recordings.

Anticipate that others will need to understand your field notes. Therefore, consistency and clarity are essential for identifying quotes, summary points, and observations. Consider using a standardized reporting form, especially as you begin your experience with taking field notes. Note the example in EXAMPLE G4 of the standardized reporting form. Field notes contain different types of information. It is essential that these different categories of information can be easily identified and organized. For example, your field notes will likely contain quotes, paraphrased quotes, summary points or themes, questions that occur to the recorder, big ideas that affect the study, observations on body language or discussion climate, and so on. Confusion can result if the type of information is not identified. It makes an enormous difference if the note is an actual quote rather than a thought passing through the head of the recorder.

Have the equipment ready, in good shape, and pretested. A number of researchers have been disappointed because they assumed that their electronic recording equipment would work correctly without testing it. Always test your electronic equipment before use, and bring extra tapes, batteries, and an extension cord. Whenever you use electronic methods, never completely trust your equipment.

We've found three exercises helpful in preparing volunteers for the recording experience. EXERCISE G1—DEMON- STRATE NOTE TAKING is basically a look over the master's shoulder. EXERCISE G2—PRACTICE TAKING FIELD NOTES is helpful but not necessarily because of the opportunity to practice. It is helpful because of the feedback given by masters as well as by other volunteers. EXERCISE G3—PRACTICE OPER- ATING EQUIPMENT must be presented carefully. Be careful to avoid implying that the volunteers lack mechanical skills, for some will be very adept. Our experience, however, shows that equipment problems are often the result of human inattention or lack of skills. Encourage volunteers to practice using the equip- ment. EXAMPLE G4—STANDARDIZED REPORTING FORM has been helpful because it provides a consistent format for recording results. We often use it when working with a team of volunteers to ensure the analyst can understand the comments.

For More Information, See Chapter 11 in *Moderating Focus Groups*

While conducting a practice focus group, gather several volunteers around the mentor, close enough to observe the note taking. The volunteers listen and observe the mentor's style and what's being recorded. The mentor will need to use sufficiently large handwrit- ing and might employ a drawing pad to improve visibility.

EXERCISE

G1—Demonstrate Note Taking

Have the volunteers practice taking field notes during the exercises in which you are demonstrating and practicing moderator skills and oral summaries. Let your volunteers conduct practice focus groups with each other on neutral, nonthreatening topics to gain experience in moderating, note taking, and oral summaries. At the conclusion of the focus group, have the note takers share what they've recorded for key points, notable quotes, big ideas, and so forth. Compare field notes. If several people are taking notes, have them trade their notes and attempt to offer a brief oral summary using someone else's field notes. Offer feedback and suggestions for improvement.

EXERCISE

G2—Practice Taking Field Notes

EXERCISE

G3—Practice Operating Equipment

While all tape recorders sort of look alike, they don't work alike. Some have lots of buttons, gauges, or dials, while others are exceedingly simple. Know your equipment, and use it several times before the focus group. You might have a short training session for all volunteers on operating the equipment. Many data have been lost by lack of attention to details, such as pushing the "play" instead of the "record" button, forgetting to turn on the microphone, not knowing how to eject or turn over the tape, or having a cord become unplugged.

EXAMPLE

G4—Standardized Reporting Form

Here's an example of a reporting form for fieldnotes taken during a focus group. We construct these using our word processors and find them very helpful with beginning recorders. Each question should fill one page.

Information About the Focus Group

Date of Focus Group	
Location of Focus Group	
Number and Description of Participants	
Moderator Name	
Asst. Moderator Name	

Responses to Questions
Q1. When you hear the term customer service, *what comes to mind?*

Brief Summary and Key Points	Notable Quotes
Comments and Observations	

Q2. *Describe exceptionally good service.*

Brief Summary and Key Points	Notable Quotes
Comments and Observations	

H. Transcribing

Volunteers can be helpful in preparing transcripts of focus groups, either during the actual groups or later, by listening to the tape recording. A volunteer with fast keyboard skills can even use a laptop computer to record the conversation during the focus group. The typist should sit close enough to hear clearly what's being said and yet far enough back from the table so as not to disturb the conversation. The ability of typists to keep up with the conversation will depend on their typing speed (at least 70 words per minute), the speed of the conversation (how fast the participants talk), the length and number of pauses in the discussion, and the complexity of the language. (TIP H3 has suggestions on transcribing during focus groups with a laptop.)

Transcribing can also take place later while listening to the tape recording of the focus group. The sound quality of focus groups is frequently poor, and the transcribing experience is less difficult when using cassette players with larger speakers or even dictation equipment with speed controls and foot-operated pedals to back up the tape. Note the suggestions in TIP H4 for preparing transcripts.

Don't assume that you will need transcripts. Transcripts are time-consuming to prepare and may not necessarily improve the quality of the analysis. If in doubt, review the volume titled *Analyzing and Reporting Focus Group Results*. Also, be careful with abridged transcripts. The abridging should be done by someone who was present in the groups and who thoroughly understands the purpose of the study. The process of abridging transcripts requires someone to make difficult judgments about the relevance of various parts of the discussion. It is a safer strategy to have volunteers transcribe everything.

Each of the two transcribing exercises has a different purpose. The first, EXERCISE H1—TRANSCRIBE DURING THE PRACTICE FOCUS GROUP, allows the research team to test the possibility of having volunteers transcribe using laptop computers during the focus group. In some circumstances, microphones just won't work, such as in places with loud background noise. In these cases, laptop transcription during the group is highly desirable. EXERCISE H2—TRANSCRIBE AFTER THE FOCUS GROUP is the actual transcription of the focus group tape. TIP H3—TIPS FOR TRANSCRIBING DURING THE FOCUS GROUP offers some useful suggestions for completing EXERCISE H1. TIP H4—TIPS FOR TRANSCRIBING AFTER THE FOCUS GROUP provides hints for volunteer transcribers that make EXERCISE H2 easier. Finally, TIP H5—TIME NEEDED

TO TRANSCRIBE A TAPE offers our rule of thumb about how much time the transcriptionist might need.

EXERCISE

H1—Transcribe During the Practice Focus Group

Invite one or more volunteers to transcribe the practice focus group using laptop computers. When the group is finished, allow the transcriber several minutes to edit and then to share results and discuss. The researcher should give thought to how intense this experience can become and how much feedback the volunteer needs or wants. Ask the volunteer how to make the exercise beneficial. It can be helpful to compare the transcript with the tape and observe omissions or differences.

EXERCISE

H2—Transcribe After the Focus Group

Because transcribing is so time-consuming, we prefer to have the volunteer practice on the real data, as opposed to practicing on a demonstration focus group. Make a backup copy of the tape, and let the volunteer transcribe the focus group. Later, when doing the analysis, the researcher can give feedback to the typist based on a comparison of the transcript and the tape.

TIP

H3—Tips for Transcribing During the Focus Group

- *Before you begin, have a hard copy of the questions in front of you, in the event the moderator skips questions. By glancing at the page, you can quickly determine the location of the question. Also, make a computer copy of the questions with a page break between questions.*
- *Before the participants arrive, determine where the typist will sit. It is best for the typist to sit several feet away from the discussion table at a small table to hold the laptop computer.*
- *Use a rapid coding system to identify participants. This could be an initial or just an assigned number corresponding to the seating position around the table. Use the number or initial to denote the speaker.*
- *Speed is important. Type as much as you can as fast as you can. You won't get everything so use dots to indicate that words are missing.*
- *Double-space between participants' comments.*
- *Don't worry about capitalizations, spelling, or punctuation. These can be added later.*
- *After the participants leave, spend some time cleaning up the transcript. Check spelling and correct capitalizations and punctuation.*

TIP

H4—Tips for Transcribing After the Focus Group

- *Use quality playback equipment. Avoid tape players with small speakers and awkward buttons. Ear-phones might be considered. If possible, use equipment with a tape speed control and foot-operated playback mechanism.*
- *Minimize distractions. Type the transcripts in a place with minimal distractions or interruptions.*
- *Identify moderator statements. Use bold print, underlining, or capitalization to identify what is said by the moderator.*

- *Identify the speakers, if possible. Type the name or code number of each speaker followed by that person's comments. This task is exceedingly difficult unless the typist was present in the actual focus group. Double-space between speakers.*
- *Type comments word for word. Don't correct grammar. Few people talk in complete sentences, and if additional words are needed to complete the thought, place these in parentheses. If words are unintelligible, then use an ellipsis [. . .] to indicate that words are missing from the transcript.*
- *Use parentheses to note special sounds that could help in analysis. Laughter, loud voices, intense comments, and so on should be noted.*

People usually underestimate the amount of time needed to transcribe an audiotape. Focus group tapes are more time-consuming to transcribe than straight dictation or speech from a single individual. In focus groups, you have multiple voices, people talking on top of each other, different levels of loudness and clarity, coupled with less than perfect sound conditions. Therefore, our rule of thumb has been that one hour of focus group takes about six to eight hours to transcribe. This assumes that the typist is experienced, familiar with the vocabulary, uses proper equipment and has no interruptions.

TIP

H5—Time Needed to Transcribe a Tape

I. Giving an Oral Summary at the End of Focus Groups

At the end of the focus group, the assistant moderator (or the moderator) offers a short oral summary of the discussion. This summary is a brief overview of the key elements of the preceding discussion. This summary serves several purposes. First, it gives participants an opportunity to verify the observations of the researcher and to expand on or modify these as needed. Second, the summary serves as a shortcut analysis strategy, if needed. Occasionally, the researchers will need to produce a summary without listening to tapes or reviewing manuscripts. In times like these, the researchers might simply transcribe the oral summary. Third, the oral summary provides an opportunity for additional discussion. After hearing the summary, focus group participants can reflect on what they've said and comment further. Sometimes, the emphasis in the summary needs to be changed, or participants realize that topics important to them were left out. Fourth, it provides an opportunity for the research team to test assumptions and interpretations.

Throughout the discussion, the assistant moderator prepares for this oral summary. In the back of his or her mind, the assistant is thinking continually about what is important to share with the participants, and this decision is guided by the purpose of the study. Disregard the question sequence, and instead begin with the most important findings. What are the important findings, and how close or far apart are the opinions? Do the participants see the issues differently or in a similar way? Keep the summary short and snappy, and use quotes to illustrate that you are building the summary on people's comments. Think about what wasn't said, and if these omitted topics are important to the purposes of the study, either ask participants why there weren't discussed or say, "I assume that these things are not important because they weren't discussed." Pause and wait for reaction from the participants. Note the discussion of how to provide an oral summary in Chapter 4 of *Moderating Focus Groups.*

Consider using EXERCISE I1—PRACTICE THE ORAL SUMMARY with the team of volunteers. You might use the questions suggested in EXAMPLE I3 —CONSUMER PRODUCT FOCUS GROUP QUESTIONS, EXAMPLE I4—PROGRAM EVALUATION FOCUS GROUP QUESTIONS, or the questions in your forthcoming study. EXERCISE I2—HAVE AN EXPERT AND A VOLUNTEER WORK AS A TEAM has been one of the most beneficial and rewarding learning experiences. However, it is also one of the most time-consuming and demanding for the expert coach. We suggest using this exercise when you are making a long-term investment in your volunteers. This exercise is helpful for improving the volunteer's skills in many areas, such as moderating and note taking, as well as presenting the oral summary. Finally, look over TIP I5—HOW TO GIVE AN ORAL SUMMARY AT THE END OF THE FOCUS GROUP, and review these points with the volunteer assistant moderators.

EXERCISE

I1—Practice the Oral Summary

Practice the oral summary during the exercises where you are also practicing moderator skills and note taking. Conduct a 20- to 30-minute focus group on a topic, and ask several volunteers to serve as assistant moderators and to offer oral summaries. After each summary, ask the focus group participants for their reactions and critiques. Note EXAMPLE I3 and EXAMPLE I4 describing a sample set of questions that can be used in practice focus groups.

EXERCISE

I2—Have an Expert and a Volunteer Work as a Team

Arrange for the volunteer to work with a coach (a master of focus groups) when conducting the first focus groups. The volunteer first observes the coach conduct a focus group; have them trade places on the second group. The coach then offers a critique. If the volunteer has already observed quality moderating and oral summaries, then the coach may just observe and critique the volunteer.

Here is a sample set of questions that can be used for many consumer products. Modify and adjust the questions as needed. The questions might be applicable to such categories as soap, breakfast cereal, fast food restaurants, automobiles, golf clubs, fishing equipment, cosmetics, deodorant, or a variety of other products. These questions can be used for practice focus groups to give moderators a chance to lead the discussion and assistants the opportunity to take field notes and provide oral summaries. You may want to have five to seven people in each focus group and a number of assistant moderators, sitting slightly back from the table.

EXAMPLE

I3—Consumer Product Focus Group Questions

1. *How and when do you use [product]?*
2. *Tell me about positive experiences you've had with [product].*
3. *Tell me about disappointments you've had with [product].*
4. *Who or what influences your decision to purchase a particular type of [product]?*
5. *When you decide to purchase [product], what do you look for? Take a piece of paper, and jot down three things that are important to you when you purchase [product].*
6. *Let's list these on the flip chart. If you had to pick only one factor that was most important to you, what would it be? You can pick something that you mentioned or something that was said by others.*
7. *Have you ever changed brands or types of [product]. What brought about the change?*
8. *Of all the things we've talked about, what is most important to you?*

When the focus group is completed, ask the assistants, one at a time, to give brief, two- or three-minute summaries. Ask those in the focus group to comment and critique the summaries.

This example contains some generic questions that could be asked in a study seeking to evaluate a program or service.

EXAMPLE

I4—Program Evaluation Focus Group Questions

1. *How have you been involved in [name of organization]?*
2. *Think back over all the years that you've participated, and tell us your fondest memory (the most enjoyable memory).*
3. *Think back over the past year of the things that [name of organization] has done. What went particularly well?*
4. *What needs improvement?*
5. *If you were inviting a friend to participate in [name of organization], what would you say in the invitation?*
6. *Suppose that you were in charge and could make one change that would make the program better. What would you do?*
7. *What can each one of us do to make the program better?*

**I5—How to Give
an Oral Summary
at the End of the
Focus Group**

1. *Before the focus group, be sure you know the key questions and the approximate time the moderator plans to spend on each key question.*
2. *Be clear in your mind about the purpose of the focus group. The summary should tie closely to this purpose.*
3. *Take notes with two things in mind: first, notes that will help you provide a brief oral summary; and, second, notes for your detailed analysis after the focus group.*
4. *Begin your oral summary with the most important findings, regardless of when they were discussed in the focus group. Don't worry about the question sequence when you construct your summary.*
5. *Begin your summary with findings—what was actually said. Attempt to capture common themes, but also acknowledge differing points of view. This descriptive summary repeats what was said but is very brief. After you've given the summary of what was said, consider offering interpretation. The interpretive summary attaches additional meaning and goes beyond the actual words.*
6. *Listen for what was not said but might have been expected. If these areas are important, then in the summary you might say, "Some things were not mentioned like . . . , and I am assuming they are not important." Look at the participants while you're saying this, and watch for reactions.*
7. *Cite key phrases used in the discussion. This demonstrates connectedness and careful listening.*
8. *Keep the summary to three minutes or less. If you ramble on, people will tune out.*
9. *When finished, look at the participants and ask, "Is this summary complete?" Or, "Does this sound accurate to you?" Or, "What would you change about this summary?"*

J. Analysis and Report Writing

Focus group analysis is a systematic process. This means that predetermined protocols are used during the focus group and continued in a sequential manner until the series of groups is completed. Also of concern is that the analysis be tailored to the problem, a process that we call "situational analysis." Simply put, the analyst waits until after the focus group to determine the analysis strategy. In some focus groups, the results are very apparent, and common themes are obvious. Preparing transcripts or even listening to the tapes may not be needed in order to write reports. In other situations, the researcher must review the field notes, tape, or even a transcript to find the central ideas. An elaborate analysis process is warranted in times of high risk or when decisions cannot be reversed. The volume on *Analyzing and Reporting Focus Group Results* provides additional suggestions.

The analysis of each focus group begins by developing a summary description of the discussion. Later, analysis across a series of focus groups involves detecting patterns or trends, identifying themes expressed by focus group participants, and attaching meaning (interpretation) to these results. Analysis improves as the analyst brings more resources to the task. These include actual firsthand observation of the focus group, field notes, oral summaries, tape recordings, and registration forms. Analysis is inseparable from report writing. In the process of preparing reports, the writer must ponder what is happening, what is important, and what meaning is attached to the discussion. These are the key ingredients of analysis. Report writing is merely an extension of the analysis process.

Because analysis spans a sizable amount of time and includes multiple tasks, the researcher should give thought as to the best role for the volunteers. The challenge is how to tap into their insights and wisdom without having them endure the time-consuming burden often associated with analysis. We've often found it helpful to discuss this task with volunteers and to receive their advice on how they would like to be involved, what they can contribute to the process, and what will be expected of them for each option.

Here are four different levels of analysis that volunteers might wish to consider:

First level—Minimal time investment. At a minimum, the volunteer observes the group and then reads and critiques the report. In such groups, the volunteer is present just to observe. He or she may take notes. In this situation, the volunteer is not truly an assistant moderator, as we have defined the role, but more of an observer. The advantage of this option is the added analysis perspective with minimal time investment required of the volunteer.

Second level—Low time investment. The next level asks that the volunteer serve in the capacity of an assistant moderator. This will require that the volunteer attend an orientation or training session on note taking, participate in the discussion of the study objectives, possibly review the questions, attend several focus groups, and read and critique reports of several focus groups.

Third level—Moderate time investment. At this level, the volunteer summarizes and prepares a report on one or more individual focus groups. The volunteer might serve as an assistant

KEY POINT

Analysis Is a Systematic Process Beginning in the First Focus Group and Continuing Through the Series of Groups

moderator or even as a moderator. She or he does all the tasks described above, plus prepares a report on each focus group. (Note the example of a completed report following the next section.)

Fourth level—Considerable time investment. This fourth level provides the volunteer with the greatest range of skills but also requires the largest amount of time. This level often involves all of the skills and responsibilities discussed in earlier steps but also asks the volunteer to prepare a report based on a series of focus groups.

We suggest five exercises to help volunteers prepare for their responsibility. These five exercises require increasing amounts of time and commitment from the volunteer. EXERCISE J1—HAVE VOLUNTEERS READ ANALYSIS REPORTS is the minimal level. EXERCISE J2—HAVE VOLUNTEERS EXAMINE THE ANALYSIS TRAIL is more difficult, but it helps the volunteer see relationships within the analysis process. EXERCISE J3—OBSERVE THE MASTER follows the traditional apprenticeship model. This model is highly effective but time-consuming. EXERCISE J4—CONDUCT ONE-GROUP ANALYSIS AND RECEIVE FEEDBACK places the volunteer in the role of the analyst but within the limited scope of a single focus group. Finally, EXERCISE J5—CONDUCT SERIES ANALYSIS WITH FEEDBACK is the most complicated and difficult of the analysis exercises. TIP J6—STRATEGY FOR GROUP ANALYSIS offers suggestions on how team members might pull their research results together.

EXERCISE

J1—Have Volunteers Read Analysis Reports

Simply by reviewing a report of a focus group, a volunteer can gain a sense of what's included and how that information is presented. Find report examples developed by researchers or other volunteers, but be sure that they are done well because they will serve as patterns.

EXERCISE

J2—Have Volunteers Examine the Analysis Trail

Here, the volunteer examines the analysis trail of a study conducted by a master. Even better than reviewing a single report is to examine the entire data stream. The volunteer may be given copies of a tape, field notes, flip charts, and the written summary for a single focus group. The volunteer can begin at either end of the data stream because the emphasis is on the continuity of parts. By beginning with the tape and field notes the volunteer gains a sense of how the information unfolds and later results in a report. By beginning with the report (at the end of the process), the volunteer can seek to verify the presence and emphasis of each concept in the fieldnotes and tape.

The volunteer observes a focus group, takes notes, and then reviews the report prepared by the master. Having experienced the group and practiced taking notes, the volunteer can then observe how the master takes the data and transforms them into a report.

EXERCISE

J3—Observe the Master

The volunteer observes a focus group, takes notes, and prepares a report. This report is critiqued by a colleague, preferably a mentor. The coach or mentor provides feedback on the extent to which the volunteer is able to identify key concepts, present ideas clearly, select quotes that illustrate important points of view, and perform other tasks necessary for quality analysis.

EXERCISE

J4—Conduct One-Group Analysis With Feedback

The volunteer observes a series of focus groups, prepares individual reports, and then writes a combined report. This is the most advanced level, the most time-consuming, and clearly the most challenging. It is often performed by the researcher; occasionally, however, a volunteer may wish to develop her or his competency by analyzing and reporting on a complete series of focus groups.

EXERCISE

J5—Conduct Series Analysis With Feedback

The research leader assembles all of the team members for a group sharing, which often lasts an entire day. At this session, each team brings a copy of its written report and also gives oral reports on each question or theme. Throughout the day, the leader encourages the participants to compare and contrast results and to identify common themes. At the end of the day, the leader guides a discussion of conclusions and recommendations.

TIP

J6—Strategy for Group Analysis

K. Oral Reporting

The guiding purpose of oral reporting is to help the listener or user of information who was not present at the focus groups to understand what took place in the discussions. Oral reports can consist of large-group presentations, small-group presentations, and one-to-one briefings. After listening to the report, listeners should feel as though they were present in the discussion. The challenge of oral reporting is to guide the listeners through the key points without confusing them with unnecessary details.

Volunteers can be enormously effective at presenting findings of focus group studies. In a number of situations, they are more convincing, trustworthy, and credible to the public and to elected decision makers than are professional staff.

You as a researcher have less control over what volunteers say and the emphasis they place on certain findings. As a result, open and honest communication with your research team becomes critical. Encourage team members to be consistent and to maintain continuity as a team. Then, trust their judgment.

One reason that volunteers are effective is that they are perceived as having less to gain, as having a degree of neutrality and a holistic perception of the problem. They are participating in research on their own time, not because of salary or benefits. Staff, by contrast, are often seen as promoting their personal or professional interests. Unfortunately, skepticism has increased about the motives, objectivity, and honesty of public employees and professional researchers.

Moreover, volunteers are known to have a tenacious loyalty to ideas and may not back away from a cause just because it lacks popularity or financial support or because someone tells them to drop the issue. Volunteers have few limits. They are not restricted to a 40-hour workweek, their enthusiasm is infectious, they can convert others to the cause, and they regularly can tap into formidable networks of other supporters.

Often, researchers overestimate the value of written reports and undervalue other forms of communications, such as person-to-person sharing of critical stories and experiences. This individual sharing between a volunteer and a decision maker may be more convincing and memorable than the most elegantly written report.

Therefore, give careful thought to the role that volunteers can play in the oral reporting. Written reports are likely to be prepared by professional staff because of the time and effort needed. The volunteers are more likely to take on the role of reviewing and critiquing the written reports. The oral report, however, is a different matter. In oral reporting, the messenger can be a critical component of the reporting mix. In part, the credibility of the report is influenced by the credibility of the reporter.

The individual sharing of reports can take on many different forms, but it is often informal, spontaneous, and variable, depending on the environment and the individuals involved. Often, it begins with a story, anecdote, or quote that is selected to illustrate an important point. Be thoughtful and purposeful about the use of stories so that they truly convey the intended point. Rehearsal and practice with the research team ensures uniform and consistent reporting. These individual reports regularly consist of three points, seamlessly woven together. Consider this style:

"Let me tell you about . . . " (story, illustration, quotation)

"This research tells us . . . " (central finding of research effort)

"Because of this, we recommend that . . . " (what needs to be done)

We suggest three exercises to help volunteers. EXERCISE K1—OBSERVE AN EXPERT GIVING AN ORAL REPORT allows the volunteer to watch and learn critical presentation skills. EXERCISE K2—PRACTICE ORAL REPORTS WITH THE TEAM is helpful to achieve consistency of messages. Remember the story of the blind men feeling different parts of an elephant and each telling a different story of what he found. It is too easy for a team to give mixed signals and inconsistent results unless the members' efforts are coordinated. Finally, EXERCISE K3—PRACTICE ONE-TO-ONE ORAL BRIEFINGS is similar to the previous exercise, except that it is less formal. BACKGROUND K4—TYPES OF ORAL REPORTS give a brief summary of the different types of oral reports.

Observe an expert giving an oral report to an individual or a group of people. Prior to the oral report, the volunteer might review the written report and think about what aspects of it she or he would present to the audience. Listen particularly to the sequence of points and the use of stories and quotes, and observe how the expert engages the audience and answers questions. If circumstances permit, invite several experts working independently to prepare oral reports. Videotape each presentation to allow for careful review and discussion. Identify the strengths of each presentation and consider developing a composite of the best features.

EXERCISE

K1—Observe an Expert Giving an Oral Report

Volunteers might practice their oral reports with the research team and invite feedback from other members of the team or from the mentor. Attempt to prepare oral reports of differing lengths, such as a brief 3- to 5-minute report, a 10- to 15-minute report, and a longer 20- to 30-minute report. In each report be certain that the key points are conveyed in a consistent manner.

EXERCISE

K2—Practice Oral Reports With the Team

Volunteers might practice giving short one-to-one oral briefings, first with the mentor and other members of the research team, then with family, friends, and colleagues, and finally with members of the target groups. This repeated practice helps ensure clarity of the message and enhances the smoothness of the delivery.

EXERCISE

K3—Practice One-to-One Oral Briefings

K4—Types of Oral Reports

Oral reports range from conversational sharing of ideas and findings to formal briefings. You may wish to involve volunteers in more than one of these reporting situations:

- Unstructured conversational report. *The unstructured conversational report is an informal and often spontaneous sharing of results. It is a hallway conversation, a coffee shop discussion, or an exchange of comments at the water cooler.*

- Structured conversational report. *The structured conversational report is planned in advance, organized in a systematic manner, but shared in an informal, one-to-one way.*

- Sponsor debriefing. *In the market research tradition, the moderator concludes the focus group and then goes behind the one-way mirror to conduct a debriefing with the sponsor.*

- Informal briefing. *The informal briefing is a short presentation to a committee or meeting. Handouts are often used. This report addresses the series of focus groups and presents the findings in an informal manner. Points are carefully organized for brevity and completeness.*

- Formal briefing. *The formal briefing is orderly, civilized, and guided by traditions and rules. Compared with the informal briefing, this type of oral report is more organized, offers less involvement for recipients, and has fewer interruptions.*

- Formal presentation/lecture/professional meeting. *The formal presentation is often used for larger groups where exact amounts of time are allocated and questions may challenge the methodology, findings, or recommendations. These presentations are typical of annual meetings and professional societies.*

NOTE: Chapter 12 of Analyzing and Reporting Focus Group Results *has more information on oral reporting.*

Final Thoughts

When the study is completed, give thought to how you will bring closure to the experience. A team of volunteers has worked with you on a journey of discovery. A lot of their lives was invested. Consider doing the following:

Acknowledge the volunteers' contributions, express your appreciation, and celebrate their accomplishments. You can do this in the form of a letter, a special event, a dinner, a certificate, and so on. Often, the most meaningful acknowledgment is the sincere and heartfelt thanks of the researcher, the study leader, and the leaders of the organization.

Review what has been learned. Reflect on what you as a researcher have learned. Consider what others have learned as well. If possible, discuss this (maybe even in a focus group) with the volunteers. Ask what went well, what needed improvement, and what was learned.

Evaluate the experience. The discussion described in the point above includes evaluative information, but you may wish to seek out and document additional factors. How much time was really needed by volunteers? What was the cost per focus group, and how would that have compared with alternatives? What are the lasting effects of the experiences in terms of the program or issue studied, the volunteers, the organization, and the community?

* * *

There is profound sense of satisfaction for the researcher when the study makes a difference. When the study is "given away" to volunteers, you greatly increase the likelihood that the study will be used. Without doubt, involving volunteers in a study and working with them can be frustrating, time-consuming, and sometimes even agonizing. However, the results are often impressive, and efforts to involve volunteers speak to a form of participatory research appropriate to a democracy. We've enjoyed opportunities to teach others and work with them in conducting focus group studies. These exercises and experiences have worked for us, and we hope they will be helpful to you. Along the way, you will probably find even better ways to teach volunteers. When you do, we'd appreciate it if you would share those insights and strategies with us.

References

Baylor, B. (1993). *Yes is better than no*. Tucson, AZ: Treasure Chest.

Cousins, J. B., & Earl, L. M., Eds. (1995). *Participatory evaluation in education: Studies in evaluation use and organizational learning*. London: Falmer.

Fetterman, D. M. (1994). Empowerment evaluation (American Evaluation Association presidential address). *Evaluation Practice, 15*(1), 1-15.

Joint Committee on Standards for Educational Evaluation (James R. Sanders, chair). (1994). *The program evaluation standards*. 2nd edition. Thousand Oaks, CA: Sage.

King, J. A., & Lonnquist, M. P. (1992). *Learning from the literature: Fifty years of action research*. Unpublished manuscript, University of Minnesota, Center for Applied Research and Educational Improvement, Minneapolis, MN.

Patton, M. Q. (1978). *Utilization-focused evaluation*. Beverly Hills, CA: Sage.

Scholtes, P. R., Joiner, B. L., & Streibel, B. J. (1993). *The team handbook*. Madison, WI: Joiner.

Stake, R. E. (1995). *Evaluating the arts in education: A responsive approach*. Columbus, OH: Charles E. Merrill.

Index to This Volume

Index to the Focus Group Kit

The letter preceding the page number refers to the volume, according to the following key:

About the Authors

Richard A. Krueger is a professor and evaluation leader at the University of Minnesota. He teaches in the College of Education and Human Development and serves as an evaluation specialist with the University of Minnesota Extension Service. He received his Ph.D. from the University of Minnesota. Over the past decade, he has taught hundreds of people to plan, conduct, and analyze focus group interviews. He's done lots  of focus groups, but he prefers teaching focus group skills to others. He has had the portunity to teach these skills to a wide variety of individuals throughout the United States as well as internationally. He loves stories. Perhaps that is what drew him to focus group interviews. Where else can one hear so many stories in such a short period of time? In addition, focus groups have enabled him to tap into the wisdom of many people. Anyone who has listened to so many focus groups is bound to absorb and benefit from the wisdom of others.

Jean A. King's biographical sketch from the University of Minnesota describes her degrees (three from Cornell, including a Ph.D.), her academic experiences (currently associate professor of educational policy and administration), and her coordination of a research and program evaluation collaborative with 40 school districts. All of this background is true and impressive, but for this book, it is of lesser importance. What's not told is that she has a deep and abiding commitment to empowering people with information. Many academics merely talk about working in the community, but Jean goes into schools and shares skills with teachers and community leaders. She has amply demonstrated her willingness to become involved in community concerns and problems.